THE GREAT BRITISH BAKE OFF

CHILDREN'S PARTY CAKES & BAKES

THE GREAT BRITISH BAKE OFF

CHILDREN'S PARTY CAKES & BAKES

70 RECIPES FOR A PERFECT CHILDREN'S PARTY

Annie Rigg

CONTENTS

INTRODUCTION

A birthday is surely one of, if not THE most important day in any child's year. Quite aside from the serious business of being one year older, there's the party to consider and the cake and treats to dream about. If you've been inspired by The Great British Bake Off and want to try your hand at some impressive bakes then this is the book to teach you how to pull off a showstopping birthday party using simple tips and techniques.

The cake is the centrepiece of most children's parties and one that your child will take great pleasure in choosing themselves, leaving you the simple task of baking it! In this book you'll find over 30 large birthday cakes for boys and girls, ranging in skill from the Space Rocket on page 84 to the Lemon Sherbet Cake (page 124) in the Simple Cakes chapter, where you'll find delicious sponge recipes that require a little less decorative skill.

It's party time and the bakes in this book are designed with fun in mind and for the home baker. The equipment required is widely available and you won't need expensive tins that will only be used once. A stand mixer will make light work of cake mixes and buttercreams, but is not essential; a hand-held electric whisk is a good second option and good old-fashioned muscle power with a mixing bowl and wooden spoon will do almost as well.

But a party is not just about the showstopping big cake. There are small cakes and biscuits to consider and savoury snacks to keep everyone happy. Cupcakes are a perennial favourite for children of all ages and can be baked in a variety of sizes to suit hands small and large. Everyone will enjoy Jam Tarts (page 138) and retro Iced Gems (page 156), and older children will take delight in S'mores Cupcakes

(page 171) and Blueberry Bakewell Slices (page 176). And there's surely no one who can resist a Doughnut (page 150) or a Chocolate Swiss Roll (page 180).

Savoury food for parties is all about small bites with maximum flavour and nibbles that can be eaten in the hand – especially when there are important games to be played and prizes to be won! Herby Sausage Rolls (page 200) are classic party food and Cheese Straws (page 196) are a sure-fire hit, but have you ever tried Hidden Hot Dogz (page 202)?

Baking for a child's party is the perfect opportunity for really letting loose with the piping bags and edible sprinkles – there's no such thing as too much in this instance. Fantastic cake decorations are now available in most supermarkets and the selection online is amazing, with sprinkles in shapes and colours to suit every theme and budget.

Where possible, the bakes in this book are decorated with edible goodies such as shortbread biscuits iced to look like sailboats, flowers and puppy dogs. Children will love to help with the decorations where they can, whether it's making chocolate jazzies for a Secret Centre Cake (page 52), spooning icing over Lemon Sprinkle Cakes (page 158) or scattering sprinkles liberally over just about anything.

Some Bake Off alumni have also contributed their favourite children's party recipes. You'll find large cakes from Holly Bell (page 92), Miranda Gore Browne (page 121) and Ian Cumming (page 126), biscuits from Cathryn Dresser (page 164) and Richard Burr (page 178), and savoury treats from Chetna Makan (page 216) and Luis Troyano (page 204).

BASICS

BAKING TIPS & TECHNIQUES

Baking for a children's party can be fun and creative, but at the same time daunting. Read the recipes ahead to make sure you don't need to start any of the elements, such as sugarpaste decorations, a day or two ahead (see the Snowman, for example, on page 49). And remember that most of the sponges for the big cakes can be made one or two days before, or even further ahead and frozen, wrapped in cling film, for up to a month.

INGREDIENTS

The recipes in this book use the simplest ingredients to create the most flavour, but follow these basic rules to ensure your bakes are at their best when they come out of the oven. See pages 12–13 for more on ingredients for decorating your cakes.

EGGS

All the recipes in this book use large free-range eggs at room temperature. If you try to add fridge-cold eggs to a light and airy creamed butter-and-sugar mixture you will find that the mixture might at best take longer to combine or, at worst, curdle. If you forget to take eggs out of the fridge in time, simply leave them in a bowl of lukewarm water for 10 minutes to warm up.

BUTTER AND DAIRY

Unless otherwise stated always, always use unsalted butter for baking. Salted butter varies in flavour enormously and will greatly affect the taste of your cakes and bakes – and not necessarily for the better.

Most of the recipes in this book call for butter that has been softened at room temperature – cakes and buttercream almost always require softened butter. Most pastry and some biscuit recipes will call for the butter to be chilled.

The same applies to other dairy products, such as milk or soured cream, which should be added to mixtures at room temperature unless stated otherwise.

EQUIPMENT

It is possible to make almost all of the cakes and bakes in this book with standard kitchen and baking equipment. Most of the cake tins used are easy to find in good kitchen shops and even some larger supermarkets.

CAKE TINS AND BAKING SHEETS

For best results in baking it is important to use good-quality, solid tins and baking sheets as they are unlikely to buckle and become misshapen in the oven. They'll conduct heat evenly, which will ensure an even rise and bake. Look out for decorative Bundt or kugelhopf tins – the better the tin, the better the result with this type and if they are non-stick then so much the better.

PIPING BAGS AND NOZZLES

Rolls of plastic disposable piping bags are indispensable. They come in a variety of sizes and are more hygienic and easier to use than traditional washable bags. The ends can be snipped to very fine points for writing or piping outlines and they fit almost all piping nozzles.

Piping nozzles are available in sets or can be bought individually, allowing you to tailor your equipment to your needs and skills. For best results, look out for nozzles made from stainless steel.

MEASURING SPOONS

The importance of measuring spoons for baking cannot be stressed enough. All the recipes in this book have been written and tested using measuring spoons. Teaspoons for stirring tea and coffee come in all shapes and sizes and using them for baking will give inconsistent results. Measuring spoons come in sets of 5 or 6, some with spoons as small as ⅛ teaspoon and going up to 1½ tablespoons.

DIGITAL SCALES

For absolute accuracy in your baking it is important to use a good set of scales. And for this they really do need to be digital. Always keep a spare battery in reserve.

BAKING PARCHMENT

Before filling, the insides of cake tins must be properly prepared. Grease the base and sides with butter and line the bases with buttered baking parchment – either a disc or a square depending on the shape of the tin. Baking parchment should not be confused with greaseproof paper – the former has a non-stick coating and will ensure that your bakes lift out of the tin or off the baking sheets easily, the latter will have the opposite effect!

OVENS AND OVEN THERMOMETERS

Oven temperatures vary across type and from brand to brand. All the recipes in this book were tested in a standard fan oven. To be sure of your oven's temperature you could use an oven thermometer, which sits on the oven shelf and gives you a secondary temperature reading. You can then adjust your oven temperature accordingly.

Always bake in the middle, or as close to the middle of the oven as possible. And when baking on more than one shelf at a time, make sure there is enough space between the shelves for your cakes to rise without hitting the shelf above.

CUTTERS

Biscuit cutters are now available in more shapes than you would have thought possible. Animals, flowers, modes of transport including cars, boats and bikes – there's a cutter for just about every eventuality. Sets of metal round and square cutters in a number of sizes and with both plain and fluted edges are a worthwhile investment. They are essential kit not only for biscuits, but also for making bite-sized pies and tarts and for cutting out sections of sponge from larger cakes.

DECORATIONS

When baking for a birthday party you can really let your imagination and creativity go wild. Piped rosettes of buttercream, a generous swoosh of brightly coloured sprinkles or a popcorn topping are fun embellishments.

COLOURS

Food-colouring pastes are used throughout this book and give a stronger colour and greater variety than the common liquid food colours found on supermarket shelves. Pastes are available singly or in sets from good baking suppliers and online. See page 21 for how to use colouring pastes to tint icings.

SPRINKLES

These come in a variety of forms, from the traditional pastel-coloured hundreds and thousands strands to tiny, vibrantly coloured nonpareils balls.

HUNDREDS AND THOUSANDS

The easiest way to brighten up a cake or bake is probably to add hundreds and thousands, and they are certainly the most widely available sprinkles, with every supermarket stocking at least one variety or colour combination. They are somewhat nostalgic, with soft, muted (and often natural) colours.

NONPAREILS

These are very similar to hundreds and thousands, but available in mixed colour combinations as bright as any rainbow. They can also be bought as single colours. They are especially useful for colour-themed projects such as the Clickety Clack Croc on page 32, or perhaps to indicate a flavour, as in the Minty Chocolate Sandwich Biscuits on page 186.

JIMMIES

Some bakes require very specific sprinkles. The Funfetti Shortbreads on page 178 and the Lemon Sprinkle Cakes on page 158 use very brightly coloured sprinkles with a light edible wax coating that are often called jimmies. Unlike standard sprinkles, which will melt and disappear into the cake, the wax coating and stronger colouring means they will hold their shape and colour during baking.

CONFETTI SUGAR SPRINKLES

Look out for these tiny discs in assorted colours – they look beautiful scattered up the sides of smoothly iced layer cakes in contrasting colours.

SUGAR BALLS, PEARLS AND DIAMONDS

These come in colours and sizes to suit almost any cake creation. Mimosa balls are simply sugar balls with a decorative textured coating. Sugar diamonds look almost like the real thing and come in several shades.

OTHER DECORATIONS

Plan ahead and you can find almost every kind of decoration online, while the confectionery aisles of larger supermarkets stock great ranges these days.

COCONUT, FLAKED ALMONDS AND POPCORN

These are a great way to add another dimension to your bakes. Flaked and desiccated coconut and flaked almonds can be found in most supermarket baking aisles. You can easily buy popcorn, but it's much more fun, and usually healthier, to pop your own. Popping kernels can be found in the snacks aisle of larger supermarkets and online.

SUGAR FLOWERS

These are easy and quick to make yourself using very small flower cutters and ready-made sugarpaste or ready-roll fondant icing. Simply roll out the icing, stamp out flowers and arrange on parchment-covered trays. Roll tiny balls of icing in contrasting colours and use a tiny dot of cold water to stick one in the centre of each flower and leave to dry overnight. They are widely available in a variety of sizes and colours from larger supermarkets or online suppliers.

SANDING SUGAR

This is simply coarsely ground sugar that comes in a variety of colours. It sparkles like sand and can be used instead of sprinkles on cakes, biscuits and Cake Pops (page 146).

EDIBLE GLITTER

This comes in a paint box of colours and adds a beautiful shimmer to bakes. Glitter should be used sparingly and be clearly labelled as edible – not to be confused with craft glitter, which can be toxic.

SWEETS AND CHOCOLATES

It's worth checking out your local sweet shop or supermarket confectionery aisle for sweets and chocolates in a variety of shapes and flavours to use as edible decorations. Confectioner's or cooking chocolate in slabs or drops is most suitable for melting. White chocolate will melt quicker than dark.

CAKE TOPPERS

Another easy and fun way to decorate your bakes is to use cake toppers. These are available for both large cakes and cupcakes and come in all shapes and sizes from paper bunting and unicorns to birthday messages on glittery banners. And, last but not least, don't forget the candles!

TEMPLATES & DIAGRAMS

SPADE TEMPLATE (PAGE 88)

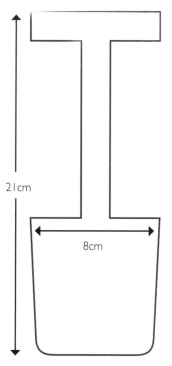

21cm

8cm

CROWN TEMPLATE (PAGE 66)

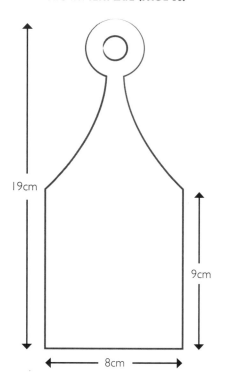

19cm

9cm

8cm

ROCKET FIN TEMPLATE (PAGE 84)

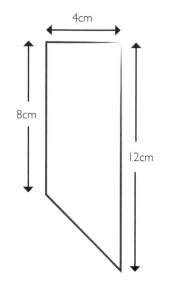

4cm

8cm

12cm

PIRATE SHIP TEMPLATE (PAGE 160)

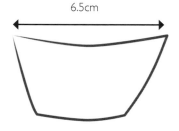

6.5cm

DOLL'S HOUSE TEMPLATE (PAGE 72)

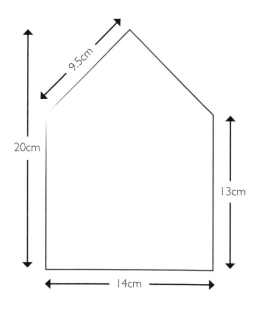

9.5cm

20cm

13cm

14cm

TENT CONSTRUCTION (PAGE 92)

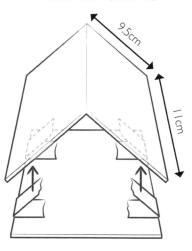

9.5cm

11cm

10cm

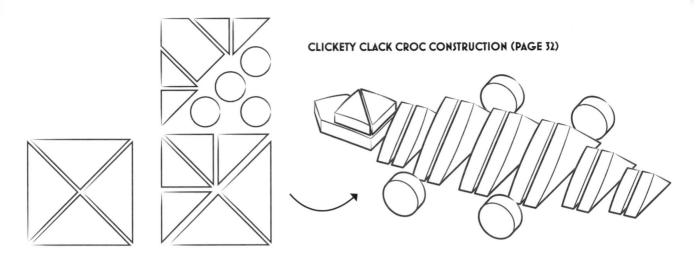

CLICKETY CLACK CROC CONSTRUCTION (PAGE 32)

DOG KENNEL & DOLL'S HOUSE CONSTRUCTION (PAGES 42 & 72)

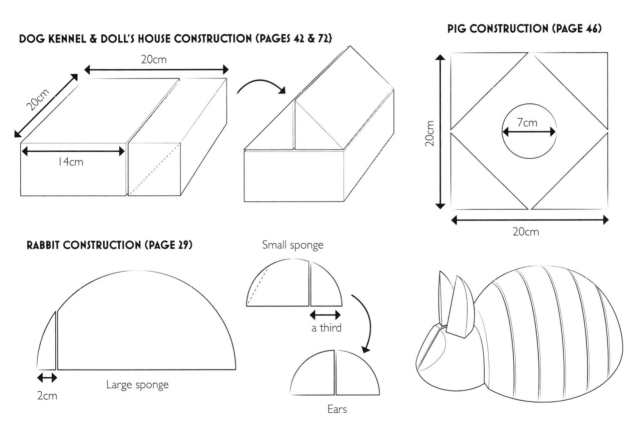

20cm

20cm

14cm

PIG CONSTRUCTION (PAGE 46)

20cm

7cm

20cm

RABBIT CONSTRUCTION (PAGE 29)

Small sponge

a third

2cm

Large sponge

Ears

BASKETWEAVE PIPING (PAGE 106)

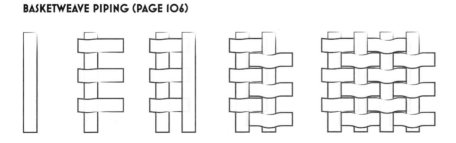

VANILLA SPONGE MIX

All too often birthday cakes are all about the fanciness, with little attention paid to the actual cake underneath all the icing and decorations. This vanilla sponge, however, is light, buttery and scented with real vanilla extract. These quantities will make cakes in a variety of shapes and sizes and make equally good cupcakes. Refer to the recipes throughout this book for the batch size you will need.

EXTRA LARGE BATCH

350g unsalted butter

350g caster sugar

2 teaspoons vanilla extract

6 eggs, lightly beaten

300g plain flour

50g cornflour

4 teaspoons baking powder

a pinch of salt

5 tablespoons milk

MEDIUM BATCH

175g unsalted butter

175g caster sugar

1 teaspoon vanilla extract

3 eggs, lightly beaten

150g plain flour

25g cornflour

2 teaspoons baking powder

a pinch of salt

2 tablespoons milk

LARGE BATCH

250g unsalted butter

250g caster sugar

2 teaspoons vanilla extract

4 eggs, lightly beaten

200g plain flour

50g cornflour

3 teaspoons baking powder

a pinch of salt

4 tablespoons milk

SMALL BATCH

100g unsalted butter

100g caster sugar

1 teaspoon vanilla extract

2 eggs, lightly beaten

100g plain flour

25g cornflour

1½ teaspoons baking powder

a pinch of salt

2 tablespoons milk

1. Preheat the oven to 180°C/160°C fan/gas mark 4 and position the shelves as close to the middle as possible, leaving enough space between them for the cakes to rise. Grease the cake tins and line the bases following the instructions in the recipe, or line a muffin tin with cases.

2. Cream the butter with the caster sugar and vanilla extract until thoroughly combined, pale and light. This will take at least 3 minutes using a stand mixer and longer if using a hand-held electric beater or a wooden spoon or spatula. Scrape down the sides of the bowl and then gradually add the beaten eggs, one at a time, mixing well between each addition.

3. Sift the flour, cornflour, baking powder and salt into the bowl, add the milk and beat until smooth, mixing slowly at first and gradually increasing the speed. Scrape down the bowl and mix again for about 30 seconds until the batter is silky smooth.

4. Divide the cake mix evenly between the prepared tins or cupcake cases and spread it level with a palette knife or the back of a spoon. Bake following the recipe instructions until golden, well risen and a skewer inserted into the centre of the sponges comes out clean. Leave to rest in the tins for 3–4 minutes and then carefully turn out onto a wire rack and leave until cold.

CHOCOLATE SPONGE MIX

A birthday party is not complete without chocolate in one form or another and surely the most often requested cake flavour is chocolate. This recipe is perfect for use in larger cakes and can be made in advance and will not come to any harm if wrapped well in cling film. If you don't feel up to making a full-on cake creation this cake will be just as delicious simply sandwiched with jam and coated in buttercream – chocolate of course.

LARGE BATCH

300g unsalted butter, softened

300g caster sugar

100g soft light brown sugar

2 teaspoons vanilla extract

6 eggs, lightly beaten

375g plain flour

80g cocoa powder

4 teaspoons baking powder

a pinch of salt

100ml whole milk

120ml boiling water

MEDIUM BATCH

100g unsalted butter

100g caster sugar

30g soft light brown sugar

1 teaspoon vanilla extract

2 eggs, lightly beaten

125g plain flour

25g cocoa powder

1½ teaspoons baking powder

a pinch of salt

2 tablespoons whole milk

3 tablespoons boiling water

1. Preheat the oven to 180°C/160°C fan/gas mark 4 and position the shelves as close to the middle as possible, leaving enough space between them for the cakes to rise. Grease the cake tins and line the bases following the instructions in the recipe.

2. Cream the butter with the caster sugar, light brown sugar and vanilla extract until thoroughly combined, pale and light. This will take at least 3 minutes using a stand mixer and longer if using hand-held electric beaters or a balloon whisk or spatula. Scrape down the sides of the bowl and then gradually add the beaten eggs, one at a time, mixing well between each addition.

3. Sift the flour, cocoa powder, baking powder and salt into the bowl, add the milk and beat until smooth, mixing slowly at first and gradually increasing the speed. Add the boiling water and scrape down the sides of the bowl. Mix again for about 30 seconds until the batter is silky smooth.

4. Divide the cake mix evenly between the prepared tins and spread it level with a palette knife or the back of a spoon. Bake as per the recipe instructions until well risen and a skewer inserted into the centre of the sponges comes out clean. Leave to rest in the tins for 3–4 minutes and then carefully turn out onto a wire rack and leave until cold before decorating.

ICED SHORTBREAD BISCUITS

Where possible, it's far more appealing to use edible decorations for your cakes and an easy way to do this is to make pretty iced biscuits. This shortbread recipe with vanilla bean paste and a touch of lemon zest is not only delicious, but also makes a crisp biscuit that will hold its shape when baked, making it ideal for decorating. You can make and bake the biscuits up to 2 days ahead and store them between layers of baking parchment in an airtight box until ready to be iced.

225g unsalted butter
150g icing sugar
1 egg, lightly beaten
grated zest of ½ unwaxed lemon
1 teaspoon vanilla bean paste
350g plain flour, plus extra for dusting
½ teaspoon baking powder
a pinch of salt

1. Cream the butter and icing sugar until pale, light and fluffy. This will be easiest and quickest using a stand mixer fitted with a paddle attachment but can also be done by hand with a wooden spoon. Scrape down the sides of the bowl with a spatula and gradually add the beaten egg, mixing well until smooth. Add the lemon zest and vanilla bean paste and mix again.

2. Sift the plain flour, baking powder and a pinch of salt into the bowl and mix until smooth. Flatten the dough into a disc, wrap it in cling film and chill for a couple of hours, or until firm. Shape and bake according to the recipe instructions.

ROYAL ICING

Royal icing sugar is the perfect icing to use for decorating shortbread or gingerbread cookies as it sets firm. Rather than using raw fresh egg whites, as in traditional recipes, shop-bought royal icing sugar includes dried egg white powder and simply needs to be mixed with water. It can be used as a super thick icing that holds its shape when piped, for example on the Iced Gems (page 156), or in a looser consistency for decorating biscuits, as described below.

Royal icing is easy to tint just about any colour of the rainbow. Paste colours are preferable to traditional food-colouring liquids as the colours are so intense that you only need to use a tiny amount each time and the little pots last for ages. Food-colouring pastes are widely available in good baking shops or online and are often sold in sets of like colours or colour palettes, as well as single colours.

Royal icing dries out quickly so keep any bowls covered with cling film when not in use. Tie the ends of filled piping bags with elastic bands or food-bag pegs between icing stages, or use closed freezer or ziplock bags until needed and simply snip the corners for piping.

TO MIX AND COLOUR ROYAL ICING

Using the ingredients listed in the recipe to guide you, tip the royal icing sugar into a bowl – it's only necessary to sift if the sugar is lumpy – and add cold water, a tablespoon at a time, mixing well between each addition until the icing is smooth, lump-free, and the desired consistency.

Use a cocktail stick or wooden skewer to add dots of colour at a time and mix well between each addition until you reach the desired shade. Colours often intensify over time so less is often more, especially if you are after bright colours.

HOW TO DECORATE BISCUITS WITH ROYAL ICING

To pipe an outline or details on biscuits the icing will need to be thick enough to hold a firm trail when the whisk is lifted from the bowl. You can always add more water if the icing is too thick, but it's impossible to take it away if you make the icing too runny and you will need to add more sugar instead.

Spoon 3 tablespoons of the icing into a disposable piping bag and push and squeeze the icing towards the end. Twist the opening of the bag to prevent any icing escaping and secure with an elastic band.

Use sharp scissors to snip a tiny hole roughly 1–2mm wide from the tip and pipe a fine continuous line around the edge of each biscuit. Leave to set for 15 minutes.

Add a drop of water to the remaining icing so that it is about the thickness of double cream and runny enough to no longer hold a ribbon trail. Use a small palette knife or teaspoon to carefully spread or 'flood' the runny icing onto the biscuit, inside the piped outline, in a smooth layer. Leave to set for 30 minutes before piping any further details onto each biscuit with the reserved piping icing.

BUTTERCREAMS & FROSTINGS

Buttercream is best made in a stand mixer fitted with the creamer or paddle attachment. It can also be made using a hand-held electric whisk, though it will take a little longer, and of course you can make it the old fashioned way, with a mixing bowl, wooden spoon and muscle power.

The standard recipes below use the quantities that are most often used throughout this book and are suitable for most big cakes or to top a batch of cupcakes. However some recipes call for more or less buttercream, and some require additional flavours, so follow the instructions given below but use the quantities listed in whichever recipe you are making.

VANILLA BUTTERCREAM

250g unsalted butter
500g icing sugar, sifted
2 teaspoons vanilla extract
2 tablespoons milk

1. Chop the butter into a bowl and beat well until pale, very soft and light – how long this takes will depend on the temperature of your butter and kitchen and how fast you beat.

2. If using a stand mixer, remove the bowl for the next stage. Gradually add the icing sugar, in 3 or 4 batches, along with the vanilla extract and milk and mix to combine using a rubber spatula. Once all the sugar has been added, return the bowl to the mixer and beat again on medium speed until light and creamy. Adding the sugar slowly by hand and away from the power source prevents the sugar dust flying all over the kitchen and making a terrific mess.

CHOCOLATE BUTTERCREAM

250g unsalted butter
500g icing sugar, sifted
75g cocoa powder, sifted
2 teaspoons vanilla extract
2–3 tablespoons milk
1 tablespoon golden syrup

1. Chop the butter into the bowl of a stand mixer or a large mixing bowl and beat until pale and light.

2. Remove the bowl from the power source, if using, and gradually add the sifted icing sugar and cocoa powder along with the vanilla extract and milk. Once all the icing sugar and cocoa powder have been incorporated, add the golden syrup and return the bowl to the mixer. Beat for a further minute or so until the mixture is light and creamy.

MERINGUE BUTTERCREAM

250g caster sugar
4 egg whites
1 teaspoon vanilla extract
a pinch of salt
325g unsalted butter

1. Tip the sugar into a large (2-litre) heatproof mixing bowl. Add the egg whites, 2 tablespoons water, the vanilla and the salt. Set the bowl over a pan of simmering water, making sure the bottom of the bowl doesn't touch the water, and use a balloon whisk to beat constantly for about 5 minutes, until the sugar has dissolved, and the meringue has doubled in volume, is warm to the touch and stiff enough to hold a firm ribbon trail.

2. Remove the bowl from the heat, scoop the mixture into the bowl of a stand mixer and whisk until the meringue is cold.

3. Gradually add the softened butter, a tablespoon at a time, whisking well to thoroughly incorporate between each addition. If the meringue is still warm when you add the butter you will almost certainly curdle the frosting. When all of the butter has been added the frosting may start to look a little curdled anyway. If this is the case, continue to whisk and it will come back together.

MERINGUE FROSTING

Work quickly with this frosting as it will start to set and become impossible to spread if it is left for too long before using.

250g caster sugar
4 egg whites
a pinch of salt

1. Put all the ingredients into a medium-sized heatproof bowl with 1 tablespoon water and set the bowl over a pan of barely simmering water, making sure the bottom of the bowl doesn't touch the water. Whisk with a balloon whisk until the sugar has completely dissolved and the mixture is foamy. Continue to cook and whisk constantly until the mixture becomes glossy white, really thick, doubles in volume and is warm to the touch and will hold a ribbon trail. This will take about 4 minutes.

2. Quickly scoop the mixture into the bowl of a stand mixer fitted with a whisk attachment and beat on a medium-high speed for a further 3 minutes, until thick, stiff and glossy.

SHOWSTOPPER CAKES

LION

*You won't need any special tins or particular skills to make this fun,
quizzical-looking lion.*

FOR THE VANILLA SPONGE

350g unsalted butter

350g caster sugar

2 teaspoons vanilla extract

6 eggs, lightly beaten

300g plain flour

50g cornflour

4 teaspoons baking powder

a pinch of salt

5 tablespoons milk

3 tablespoons raspberry or apricot jam

FOR THE VANILLA BUTTERCREAM

400g unsalted butter

800g icing sugar, sifted, plus 4 tablespoons

2 teaspoons vanilla extract

4–5 tablespoons milk

3 tablespoons cocoa powder, sifted

1 tablespoon golden syrup

FOR THE DECORATION

yellow and black food-colouring pastes

200g ready-roll fondant icing

2 tablespoons white nonpareils sprinkles

chocolate sprinkles

icing sugar, for dusting

YOU WILL ALSO NEED

2 x 23cm round cake tins

1 x 6-hole muffin tin

2 x paper cupcake cases

2 x disposable piping bags

open star nozzle

MAKE THE VANILLA SPONGE

1. Preheat the oven to 180°C/160°C fan/gas mark 4
and position the shelves as close to the middle as possible,
leaving enough space between them for the cakes to
rise. Grease the cake tins and line the bases with discs
of buttered baking parchment. Line 2 of the holes in the
muffin tin with paper cupcake cases.

2. Make the vanilla sponge mix following the instructions
on page 16, up to the end of step 3.

3. Half fill the cupcake cases with the cake mix and divide
the rest evenly between the prepared tins, spreading it
level with a palette knife or the back of a spoon. Bake the
cupcakes for about 15 minutes and the large cakes for
about 30 minutes, until golden, well risen and a skewer
inserted into the centre of the cakes comes out clean.
Leave to rest in the tins for 3–4 minutes and then
carefully turn out onto a wire rack and leave until cold.

ASSEMBLE THE CAKE

4. Make the vanilla buttercream following the instructions on page 22, reserving the 4 tablespoons icing sugar, the cocoa powder and the golden syrup.

5. Spoon two-thirds of the buttercream into a separate bowl and add the cocoa powder and golden syrup. Mix well until smooth and thoroughly combined.

6. Use a large serrated knife to level the tops of the sponge layers. Place one layer on a serving plate and spread the top with 2 tablespoons of jam. Spread the underside of the second layer with 2–3 tablespoons of vanilla buttercream and sandwich the two together.

7. Tint the remaining vanilla buttercream pale yellow and use a palette knife to spread it over the top of the cake. Spread half the chocolate buttercream over the sides in a smooth, even layer. Spoon the remaining chocolate buttercream into a large piping bag fitted with an open star nozzle.

8. Unwrap the cupcakes and cut them in half horizontally – you will only need the bottom half of each cupcake. Spread the top and sides of each small round cake with jam.

DECORATE THE LION

9. Take half the fondant icing and wrap the rest in cling film. Cut it in half again and roll each piece out on a lightly dusted work surface to a neat circle 4cm wider than the cupcakes. Cover the top and sides of each small cake and trim the bottom edges to neaten them. Lightly brush the tops with water and cover them with white nonpareils sprinkles. Position on top of the large cake to make the lion's muzzle.

10. Pipe ribbons of the chocolate buttercream all around the edge of the cake to create the lion's mane. Repeat to make a double-height layer of buttercream and scatter with chocolate sprinkles.

11. Take half the remaining fondant icing and colour it black. Split it in half and roll 2 small pupils for the eyes from one half and a larger nose from the other half. Squeeze the nose into a triangle shape and place it just above the lion's muzzle.

12. Roll the remaining white fondant into 2 eyeballs, flatten them slightly and place on top of the cake. Slightly flatten the pupils, brush the undersides with water and position them on top of the eyes.

13. Mix the remaining 4 tablespoons of icing sugar with a little water and black food-colouring paste to make a thick writing icing and spoon into a disposable piping bag. Snip the end to a fine point and pipe a mouth and 2 eyebrows onto the lion's face. Scatter chocolate sprinkles around the base of the cake and then leave to set for 1 hour before serving.

YOU CAN NOW BUY TUBES OF WRITING ICING THAT ARE IDEAL FOR FIDDLY ICING TWIDDLES.

BUNNY RABBIT

SERVES 12

A cute cake that could be coated in chocolate buttercream (page 23) and milk chocolate curls if you prefer.

FOR THE VANILLA SPONGE

350g unsalted butter

350g caster sugar

2 teaspoons vanilla extract

6 large eggs, lightly beaten

300g plain flour

50g cornflour

4 teaspoons baking powder

a pinch of salt

5 tablespoons milk

400g raspberry jam

FOR THE VANILLA BUTTERCREAM

250g unsalted butter

500g icing sugar, sifted

2 teaspoons vanilla bean paste

2 tablespoons milk

FOR THE DECORATION

200g white chocolate

pink hundreds and thousands

1 x pink and 2 x brown sugar-coated chocolate drops, for the eyes and nose

YOU WILL ALSO NEED

2-litre ovenproof bowl

250ml ovenproof bowl

2 x cocktail sticks

MAKE THE VANILLA SPONGE

1. Preheat the oven to 180°C/160°C fan/gas mark 4 and position the shelf in the middle. Butter the insides of the bowls and line the base of each with a small disc of baking parchment.

2. Make the vanilla sponge mix following the instructions on page 17, up to the end of step 3.

3. Scoop the cake mix into the small bowl to two-thirds full and the remaining mixture into the larger bowl. Level the tops with a spatula or the back of a spoon. Bake both bowls on the middle shelf of the oven for 25–30 minutes for the smaller bowl, and 70 minutes for the larger one, until both cakes are well risen, golden brown and a skewer inserted into the centres comes out clean. Leave to rest in the bowls for 4–5 minutes and then carefully turn out onto a wire rack and leave until completely cold. Wrap in cling film and set aside.

PREPARE THE DECORATIONS

4. Make the vanilla buttercream following the instructions on page 22. Chill until ready to use.

5. Use a vegetable peeler or the coarse side of a box grater to make white chocolate shavings. Chill until ready to use.

ASSEMBLE THE CAKE

6. Using the diagram on page 15 as a guide, assemble the cake pieces. Unwrap the larger cake and place it on a chopping board on its side. If it has domed in the oven, use a large serrated knife to trim the flat edge level and sit it on the board. Trim a 2cm slice from one edge of the cake – this is where the head will join the rabbit's body. Slice the trimmed dome vertically into 6 even slices and spread the cut sides with jam. Sandwich the dome back together.

7. Place the large dome on a cake board and use a spatula to cover it with about two-thirds of the buttercream. Press two-thirds of the white chocolate shavings all over the buttercream.

8. Unwrap the smaller cake, trim the flat edge to level it and sit it on the board. Slice off one-third from the side of the cake and set it aside. Carefully shave a little sponge from the opposite side of the dome to shape a pointed nose. Cut the cake in half from the nose to the back of the head, spread with jam and sandwich back together.

9. Press the small cake up against the larger cake to join the head to the body and cover the head with half the remaining buttercream and half the white chocolate shavings.

10. To make the ears, take the section of sponge you cut away from the head and cut it in half to make 2 ear shapes. Cover with half the remaining buttercream and chocolate shavings and then sprinkle the front of each ear with pink hundreds and thousands. Insert a cocktail stick into the base of each ear.

11. Carefully press the ears into the top of the bunny's head. Press brown sugar-coated chocolate drops into position for the eyes and a pink one for the nose. Roll the remaining buttercream into a ball, coat it in the remaining white chocolate shavings and position as a tail.

CLICKETY CLACK CROC

SERVES 12–16

You'll need to plan in advance where you want to serve this cake from as it is easier to finish icing the sections when they are in position. See page 15 for diagrams of how to cut out and assemble the cake shapes.

FOR THE VANILLA SPONGE

350g unsalted butter

350g caster sugar

2 teaspoons vanilla extract

6 eggs, lightly beaten

300g plain flour

50g cornflour

4 teaspoons baking powder

a pinch of salt

5 tablespoons milk

400g raspberry or apricot jam

FOR THE VANILLA BUTTERCREAM

400g unsalted butter

800g icing sugar, sifted

2 teaspoons vanilla bean paste or extract

4 tablespoons milk

FOR THE DECORATION

light and dark green, yellow and black food-colouring pastes

50g white fondant icing

strawberry liquorice laces

light and dark green nonpareils sprinkles

YOU WILL ALSO NEED

3 x 20cm square cake tins

6cm round cutter

2 or 3 baking sheets

disposable piping bag

open star nozzle

MAKE THE VANILLA SPONGE

1. Preheat the oven to 180°C/160°C fan/gas mark 4 and position the shelves as close to the middle as possible, leaving enough space between them for the cakes to rise. Grease the cake tins and line the bases with squares of buttered baking parchment.

2. Make the vanilla sponge mix following the instructions on page 17, up to the end of step 3.

3. Divide the cake mix evenly between the prepared tins and spread it level with a spatula or the back of a spoon. Bake for 25–30 minutes or until well risen, golden brown and a skewer inserted into the centre of the cakes comes out clean. Leave to rest in the tins for 4–5 minutes and then carefully turn out onto a wire rack and leave until cold.

CUT THE PIECES FOR THE CROCODILE

4. Use the diagram on page 15 to help you cut the sponge layers into several triangles and circles. First use a large serrated knife to cut each cake in half diagonally, corner to corner, to give 6 large sponge triangles. Cut 3 of these large triangles in half again to make 6 even-sized triangles and set them aside.

5. Use the cutter to stamp out 4 discs from one of the large triangles and discard the trimmings. Set aside.

6. Take another large triangle and cut notches at the centre of each edge. Cut from point to point to make 4 medium triangles. Set aside.

7. Take the final large triangle and cut 2 notches along the long edge, one-third and two-thirds of the way along. Cut at right-angles from these notches to make one arrow-shaped piece and 2 triangles. Cut the triangles through the middle to make 4 small triangles. Set aside.

ASSEMBLE THE CROC

8. Make the vanilla buttercream following the instructions on page 22. Line a baking sheet with baking parchment.

9. Use a little jam to sandwich the large triangles together in pairs, flat sides together. Stand them upright on a baking sheet, long edges down, and spread with a thin crumb coat layer of buttercream. Repeat with the medium triangles and 2 of the small triangles.

10. Take the final small triangles and use a little jam to stick them together at the long edges to make a square. Stick this flat against the square end of the arrow-shaped piece to make the croc's head. Coat the whole head in buttercream. Chill all the pieces for 30 minutes to set.

11. Spoon 6 tablespoons of buttercream into a small bowl and tint it yellow using food-colouring paste. Use a palette knife to cover the round sponge pieces in a thin crumb coat of buttercream and return to the fridge for 30 minutes. Cover the remaining yellow buttercream in cling film to stop it drying out.

12. Divide the remaining plain buttercream between 2 bowls and colour each a different shade of green. Spread the sides of 2 of the big triangles, 1 of the small triangles and the whole head in a thick layer of the darker shade of green. Spread the sides of the remaining triangles in the lighter green. Spread the remaining yellow buttercream over the wheels. Chill all the pieces for another 30 minutes.

13. Place the lighter green large triangle in the centre of a long cake board or directly onto the serving table on an oilcloth tablecloth. Place the darker large triangles either side, leaving a small gap between each section. Position the medium triangles at either end. Place the head at one end

IF DINOSAURS ARE YOUR PREFERRED SNAPPY CREATURES THEN TRY TINTING THE BUTTERCREAM TONES OF BROWN AND GREY INSTEAD.

and the small triangle at the opposite end to make a tail. Position the yellow wheels either side.

14. Scoop the remaining light green buttercream into a piping bag fitted with a star nozzle and pipe rosettes across the tops of the lighter sections. Repeat with the darker green buttercream.

15. Pinch off 2 cherry sized pieces of sugarpaste, roll them into balls and press them into discs. Pinch off 2 pea-sized pieces of sugarpaste and tint them black using food-colouring paste. Roll them into balls and press them into discs. Use a dab of water to attach the black discs to the white ones to make eyes and press them into the buttercream on either side of the crocodile's nose. Divide the remaining sugarpaste into 12 even-sized pieces. Roll them into balls and position one between each section of the crocodile to resemble joining pieces.

17. Place a long liquorice lace at the crocodile's mouth for a string and scatter the tops of the cake pieces with light and dark green nonpareils sprinkles to serve.

RUBBER DUCK

SERVES 16–20

You'll need to buy a selection of rubber ducks in assorted sizes for this cake – the ones from your own bath tub really won't do! Meringue buttercream topped with sugar pearls gives the top of this cake a real bubbly bath appearance.

FOR THE VANILLA SPONGE

350g unsalted butter

350g caster sugar

2 teaspoons vanilla extract

6 eggs, lightly beaten

300g plain flour

50g cornflour

4 teaspoons baking powder

a pinch of salt

5 tablespoons milk

6–8 tablespoons jam, any flavour

FOR THE MERINGUE BUTTERCREAM

250g caster sugar

4 egg whites

1 teaspoon vanilla extract

a pinch of salt

325g unsalted butter

FOR THE DECORATION

1kg ready-roll fondant icing

blue food-colouring pastes in various shades

white sugar pearls

icing sugar, for dusting

YOU WILL ALSO NEED

2 x 23cm round cake tins

string, for measuring

plain round cutters in different sizes

disposable piping bag

plain nozzle

small rubber ducks

MAKE THE VANILLA SPONGE

1. Preheat the oven to 180°C/160°C fan/gas mark 4 and position the shelves as close to the middle as possible, leaving enough space between them for the cakes to rise. Grease the cake tins and line the bases with discs of buttered baking parchment.

2. Make the vanilla sponge mix following the instructions on page 17, up to the end of step 3.

3. Divide the batter evenly between the prepared tins and spread it level with a palette knife or the back of a spoon. Bake for 30–35 minutes until golden, well risen and a skewer inserted into the centre of the cakes comes out clean. Leave to rest in the tins for 3–4 minutes and then carefully turn out onto a wire rack and leave until cold.

ASSEMBLE THE CAKE

4. Make the meringue buttercream following the instructions on page 23.

5. Using a long serrated knife, trim the tops of the cakes to level them and cut each one in half horizontally. Lay one of the bottom slices on a cake board and spread it with a third of the jam. Spread about a fifth of the buttercream over the jam and sandwich with another cake layer. Repeat three times and then cover the whole cake with half the remaining buttercream – you want an even, thin crumb coat layer that covers the entire sponge.

DECORATE THE CAKE

6. Tint 750g of the ready-roll icing the palest shade of blue using a cocktail stick dipped into the food-colouring paste and knead until smooth and an even colour.

7. Roll out the blue fondant on a lightly dusted work surface to make a long strip the same length as the circumference of the cake and 2cm wider than its height. It is easy to measure this using a length of string. Trim the ends to neaten them and roll up the icing into a tight roll. Hold the icing against the side of the cake with the bottom edges lined up and, starting at one of the short ends, carefully unroll it around the cake to cover it smoothly. Lightly moisten the join with a little water to seal. Roll the excess icing at the top down to create the effect of a roll-top bath.

8. Divide the remaining icing into 3 and tint 2 of the portions different shades of blue. Leave the third portion white.

9. Roll out the white icing to about 1mm thick and use the cutters to stamp out discs in assorted sizes. Repeat with the blue icings. Very lightly brush the discs with water and press them around the sides of the cake to look like bubbles.

10. Scoop the remaining buttercream into a piping bag fitted with a plain nozzle and pipe little spheres of frosting to resemble bubbles all over the top of the cake. Pipe a mound of bubbles to one side of the bathtub and some more spilling onto the cake board. Scatter with sugar pearls and sit the rubber ducks among the bubbles to serve.

USE A COCKTAIL STICK TO ADD FOOD COLOURING TO THE ICING IN TINY AMOUNTS. A LITTLE COLOURING GOES A LONG WAY AND IT'S FAR EASIER TO ADD COLOUR THAN TO TAKE IT AWAY.

YOU CAN OF COURSE MAKE FONDANT OR MARZIPAN RUBBER DUCKS IF YOU FEEL LIKE BEING CREATIVE.

BIRD'S NEST

SERVES 12

Sugarpaste flowers are easy to find in shops that sell cake and baking supplies, or online. Pretty sugar-coated eggs in assorted colours and sizes are easier to find around Easter time, which makes this a wonderful springtime birthday cake.

FOR THE VANILLA SPONGE

250g unsalted butter

250g caster sugar

2 teaspoons vanilla extract

4 eggs, lightly beaten

200g plain flour

50g cornflour

3 teaspoons baking powder

a pinch of salt

4 tablespoons milk

6 tablespoons seedless raspberry or apricot jam

FOR THE CHOCOLATE BUTTERCREAM

250g unsalted butter

500g icing sugar, sifted

75g cocoa powder, sifted

2 tablespoons milk

1 tablespoon golden syrup

2 teaspoons vanilla extract

FOR THE DECORATION

100g dark chocolate, chopped

75g milk chocolate, chopped

100g shredded wheat biscuit cereal, lightly crushed

milk chocolate-coated stick biscuits

sugarpaste flowers in different sizes

assorted sugar-coated chocolate eggs

YOU WILL ALSO NEED

2 x 20cm round cake tins

1 x 18cm round cake tin

12cm plain round cutter

disposable piping bag

bird decorations

MAKE THE VANILLA SPONGE

1. Preheat the oven to 180°C/160°C fan/gas mark 4 and position the shelves as close to the middle as possible, leaving enough space between them for the cakes to rise. Grease the cake tins and line the bases with discs of buttered baking parchment.

2. Make the vanilla sponge mix following the instructions on page 17, up to the end of step 3.

3. Divide the cake mix evenly between the prepared tins and level them with a palette knife or the back of a spoon. Bake for 20 minutes until golden, well risen and a skewer inserted into the centres comes out clean. Leave to rest in the tins for 3–4 minutes and then carefully turn out onto a wire rack and leave until cold.

ASSEMBLE THE CAKE

4. Make the chocolate buttercream following the instructions on page 23.

5. Lay the sponge layers on the work surface and level the tops, if necessary, using a large serrated knife. Spread one of the big layers with half the jam. Spoon a third of the buttercream into a large disposable piping bag and snip the end to make a 1cm hole. Pipe the buttercream on top of the jam in an even layer and spread it smooth using a palette knife. Place the second big layer on top and spread it with the remaining jam and half the remaining buttercream.

6. Use the round cutter to cut out a circle from the middle of the smaller cake. Lay the sponge ring on top of the other cake layers and cover the whole cake in the rest of the buttercream, creating texture with the palette knife.

DECORATE THE NEST

7. Melt all the chocolate and the butter in a heatproof bowl over a pan of barely simmering water, making sure the bottom of the bowl doesn't touch the water, or in the microwave on a low setting. Stir until smooth and leave to cool for 5 minutes.

8. Tip the crushed shredded wheat into the melted chocolate, stir to coat and press onto the sponge ring to form a bird's nest shape. Leave to set.

9. Break the chocolate-coated biscuit sticks into pieces and scatter them around the base of the cake to look like twigs. Press sugarpaste flowers around the sides, fill the nest with eggs and place a few feathered birds on top before serving.

DOG KENNEL

SERVES 12

Biscuit cutters are now available in more shapes than you would have thought possible and when it comes to dog shapes you can find a cutter to suit most breeds! Match the biscuits that decorate this cake to your family pet, but don't forget to add their ball and a little bowl of their favourite food.

FOR THE VANILLA SPONGE

350g unsalted butter

350g caster sugar

2 teaspoons vanilla extract

6 eggs, lightly beaten

350g plain flour

4 teaspoons baking powder

4 tablespoons milk

6 tablespoons raspberry or apricot jam

FOR THE VANILLA BUTTERCREAM

300g unsalted butter

600g icing sugar

6 tablespoons milk

2 teaspoons vanilla extract

75g cocoa powder

FOR THE SHORTBREAD BISCUITS

125g unsalted butter

75g icing sugar

1 egg yolk

1 teaspoon vanilla bean paste

175g plain flour, plus extra for dusting

¼ teaspoon baking powder

a pinch of salt

FOR THE DECORATION

250g royal icing sugar

brown and black food-colouring pastes

100g desiccated coconut

200g dark chocolate, chopped

150g white chocolate, chopped

1 x tube red writing icing

chocolate sprinkles

yellow mimosa balls

YOU WILL ALSO NEED

2 x 20cm square cake tins

1 x 6-hole bun tin

7½–8cm plain round cookie cutter

dog-shaped cutters

disposable piping bag

MAKE THE VANILLA SPONGE

1. Preheat the oven to 180°C/160°C fan/gas mark 4 and position the shelves as close to the middle as possible, leaving enough space between them for the cakes to rise. Grease the cake tins and line the bases with squares of buttered baking parchment.

2. Make the vanilla sponge mix following the instructions on page 17, up to the end of step 3.

3. Divide the cake mix evenly between the prepared tins and spread it level with a palette knife or the back of a spoon. Bake for 20–25 minutes until golden, well risen and a skewer inserted into the centre of the sponges comes out clean. Leave to rest in the tins for 3–4 minutes and then carefully turn out onto a wire rack and leave until cold.

MAKE THE DOG, BOWL AND NAME PLAQUE BISCUITS

4. Make the shortbread dough following the instructions on page 20. Wrap in cling film and chill for 1 hour, until firm. Line the baking sheets with baking parchment. Grease 3 of the bun tin holes.

5. Roll out the chilled dough on a lightly floured surface to 2–3mm thick. Use the dog-shaped cutters to stamp out 2–4 dog-shaped biscuits and then use a sharp knife to cut a 1 x 6cm strip for the name plaque. Arrange the pieces on the prepared baking sheets. Use the round cutter to stamp out 1–3 discs and use them to line the greased bun holes. Chill again for 15 minutes.

6. Bake the chilled biscuits for about 12 minutes, until golden brown. Leave to cool on the trays.

DECORATE THE BISCUITS

7. Prepare the royal icing following the instructions on page 21, adding enough water to make a stiff writing icing. Spoon 3 tablespoons into a disposable piping bag and cover the remainder with cling film. If you are making a brown-haired dog, use food-colouring paste to tint the icing brown. Snip the end of the bag to a fine point and, using the detailed instructions on page 21 to help you, pipe an outline around the edge of the dog cookies and the name plaque. Leave to set for 15 minutes.

8. Add a drop of water to the remaining icing and tint some, or all of it, using food-colouring paste. Flood the dog shapes and name plaque with the icing and leave to dry for 3–4 minutes.

9. Meanwhile, prepare the hair for your dogs. For scruffy brown hair, tip the coconut into a bowl, add a small amount of food-colouring paste on the end of a skewer or cocktail stick and mix through with your hands until the coconut is an even colour in your desired shade. Scatter the coconut – either brown or plain white – over the still-wet royal icing.

10. Pipe little white dots of royal icing for eyes and then tint some of the icing black to finish the eyes and pipe noses and dog collars.

ASSEMBLE THE CAKE

11. Make the vanilla buttercream following the instructions on page 22 and using 4 tablespoons of the milk. Scoop out half the buttercream and set it aside. Add the cocoa powder and an extra 2 tablespoons milk to the remaining buttercream and beat until smooth.

12. Using a large serrated knife and the diagram on page 15 to help you, cut 2 of the sponge layers into 20 x 14cm rectangles. Cut these layers in half horizontally to make 4 even slices. Place one slice on a serving plate and spread the top with jam. Top with a second slice and spread with buttercream. Repeat, alternating the jam with the buttercream.

13. Take one of the reserved small sections of sponge and cut it in half diagonally to make two 20cm-long triangular wedges. Sit the 2 triangles side by side to make a pitched roof. Spread a little jam along the long side to stick them together and place on top of the cake stack. You will not need the last piece of cake for this recipe.

14. Cover the whole cake with a thin, even crumb coat layer of buttercream and chill for 15 minutes.

MAKE THE CHOCOLATE ROOF AND WALL PANELS

15. Meanwhile, cover 2 baking sheets with baking parchment. Melt the dark chocolate in a heatproof bowl set over a pan of barely simmering water, making sure the bottom of the bowl doesn't touch the water, or in the microwave on a low setting. Stir until smooth and remove

from the heat, then pour over one of the prepared baking sheets and use a palette knife to spread to an even 1–2mm thick. Transfer to the fridge to set for 10 minutes. Repeat with the white chocolate. It may not take as long to melt.

16. Use a long-bladed knife to cut the dark chocolate into 1cm strips the same height as the walls of the kennel. Cut the white chocolate into 1cm strips the same length as each side of the pitched roof. Chill until needed.

DECORATE THE CAKE

17. Use a palette knife to cover the sides of the cake with an even layer of chocolate buttercream. Cover the roof section with vanilla buttercream. Use a clean palette knife to lift the dark chocolate panels from the paper and arrange them around the walls of the kennel. Arrange the white chocolate panels over the top to make a roof.

18. Pipe your dog's name onto the plaque using the tube of red writing icing and press it into the buttercream at the front of the kennel. Decorate the ridge of the roof with more red icing.

19. Arrange the dog-shaped biscuits and bowls around the kennel, fill the bowls with chocolate sprinkles and give one of your dogs a yellow mimosa tennis ball.

WHEN MELTING CHOCOLATE IN THE MICROWAVE ALWAYS CHOP IT INTO SMALL PIECES AND HEAT IT ON SHORT BURSTS ON A LOW SETTING, STIRRING IN BETWEEN BURSTS TO MELT EVENLY.

PIGGY-WIG

SERVES 12–16

With his cheeky grin and marshmallow eyes, this little piggy is sure to please smaller children.

FOR THE ROUND VANILLA SPONGES

350g unsalted butter

350g caster sugar

2 teaspoons vanilla extract

6 eggs, lightly beaten

300g plain flour

50g cornflour

4 teaspoons baking powder

a pinch of salt

5 tablespoons milk

6 tablespoons raspberry jam

FOR THE SQUARE VANILLA SPONGE

125g unsalted butter

125g caster sugar

2 eggs, lightly beaten

100g plain flour

25g cornflour

1½ teaspoons baking powder

2 tablespoons milk

FOR THE VANILLA BUTTERCREAM

250g unsalted butter

500g icing sugar, sifted

2 teaspoons vanilla extract

4 tablespoons milk

pink food-colouring paste

FOR THE DECORATION

3 tablespoons pink nonpareils sprinkles

2 mini pink marshmallows

2 white marshmallows

1 x tube black writing icing

YOU WILL ALSO NEED

2 x 23cm round cake tins

1 x 20cm square cake tin

7cm round cutter

MAKE THE VANILLA SPONGES

1. Preheat the oven to 180°C/160°C fan/gas mark 4 and position the shelves as close to the middle as possible, leaving enough space between them for the cakes to rise. Grease the cake tins and line the bases with buttered baking parchment.

2. Make the first batch of sponge mix for the round sponges following the instructions on page 17, up to the end of step 3. Divide the batter evenly between the prepared round cake tins and spread it level with a palette knife or the back of a spoon. Bake for about 30 minutes until golden, well risen and a skewer inserted into the centre of the sponges comes out clean. Leave to rest in the tins for 3–4 minutes and then carefully turn out onto a wire rack and leave until cold.

3. Make the second batch of cake mix following the same method and bake in the square tin for 20–25 minutes.

A CRUMB COAT IS A THIN LAYER OF ICING THAT COVERS THE CAKE TO SEAL IN THE CRUMBS. IT IS FOLLOWED BY A SECOND LAYER OF ICING THAT FINISHES THE CAKE.

YOU COULD USE FREEZE-DRIED RASPBERRY POWDER TO ADD FLAVOUR AND COLOUR TO THIS CAKE IF YOU'D RATHER NOT USE FOOD COLOURING.

ASSEMBLE THE CAKE

4. Make the buttercream following the instructions on page 22. Tint the buttercream pink using food-colouring paste.

5. Use a large serrated knife to level the tops of the round sponges. Place one layer on a serving plate and spread the top with jam. Spread the underside of the second layer with 2–3 tablespoons of buttercream and sandwich the two together. Cover the cake with a thin crumb coat of buttercream, spreading it smooth with a palette knife. Chill for 20 minutes.

6. Using the diagram on page 15 as a guide, lay the square sponge on a chopping board and use the round cutter to stamp out a 7cm disc from the centre – this will be the snout. Cut the 4 corners of the square into even triangles. Discard the trimmings or use them for something else.

7. Spread the tops of 2 of the triangles with jam and top each with a second triangle – these will be the piggy's ears. Cover the top and sides of each ear and the snout in a thin crumb coat of buttercream. Chill for 20 minutes.

DECORATE THE PIGGY

8. Cover the top and sides of the large cake, ears and snout with buttercream, spreading it smoothly and evenly with a palette knife. Press pink sugar sprinkles over the top of each ear.

9. Position the ears either side of the pig's head. Place the snout on top and press the mini marshmallows into it to make nostrils. Position the large marshmallows as eyes and then pipe pupils and a mouth using the tube of black writing icing to finish.

SNOWMAN

SERVES 24–30

This guy is perfect for a winter birthday. You will need to make the sugarpaste decorations 2–3 days ahead of the party to give them plenty of time to dry. You also need to bake the cake in two batches, so plan ahead!

FOR THE VANILLA SPONGE (2 BATCHES)

2 × 350g unsalted butter
2 × 350g caster sugar
2 × 2 teaspoons vanilla extract
2 × 6 eggs, lightly beaten
2 × 300g plain flour
2 × 50g cornflour
2 × 4 teaspoons baking powder
2 × a pinch of salt
2 × 5 tablespoons milk
400g raspberry jam

FOR THE VANILLA BUTTERCREAM

200g unsalted butter
400g icing sugar
2 tablespoons milk
1 teaspoon vanilla extract

FOR THE MERINGUE FROSTING

250g caster sugar
4 egg whites
a pinch of salt

FOR THE DECORATION

200g sugarpaste
red, black, orange and blue food-colouring pastes
milk chocolate-coated stick biscuits
blue sugar-coated chocolate drops
ribbon or knitting for a scarf
icing sugar
white chocolate-coated coconut and almond balls

YOU WILL ALSO NEED

1 × 2-litre heatproof bowl
1 × 250ml heatproof bowl
plain round cutters – 6cm, 7cm and 10cm

MAKE THE SUGARPASTE DECORATIONS

1. Two or three days before you plan to serve the cake, tint half the sugarpaste red, knead it until smooth and the colour is evenly incorporated throughout, then divide into 3. Roll out 1 piece on a sheet of baking parchment to a neat circle and use a 10cm cutter to stamp out a disc. Stamp out a 7cm circle from the second piece and place both on a clean sheet of parchment.

2. Roll the remaining red sugarpaste into a strip 12cm long and the same width as the 6cm cookie cutter. Trim the long sides to neaten them and wrap the strip around the cutter. Press the ends together to seal them and set aside on the baking parchment.

3. Break off a cherry sized nugget of white sugarpaste, tint it blue and set it aside, wrapped in cling film. Break off another cherry sized nugget and tint it black. Split it in half, roll it into 2 balls and place them on the baking parchment. Tint the remaining sugar paste orange and mould it into a carrot shape. Leave all the pieces to dry for at least 48 hours.

MAKE THE VANILLA SPONGES

4. The next day, preheat the oven to 180°C/160°C fan/gas mark 4. Butter the heatproof bowls and lightly dust them with plain flour.

5. You're going to make 2 batches of vanilla sponge. Make the first batch following the instructions on page 17, up to the end of step 3.

6. Spoon the cake mix into the 2 prepared bowls, filling them half to two-thirds full and spreading them level with a spatula or the back of a spoon. Bake for about 30 minutes for the smaller cake and 1 hour for the larger cake, until golden, well risen and a skewer inserted into the centre of the sponges comes out clean. Leave to rest in the bowls for 3–4 minutes and then carefully turn out onto a wire rack to cool.

7. Make the second batch of sponge mix. Wash the bowls, butter and flour them and bake a second batch of sponges, as above. When all the cakes are completely cold, wrap them in cling film and leave them overnight.

ASSEMBLE THE CAKE

8. Make the vanilla buttercream following the instructions on page 22.

9. Use a large serrated knife to level the flat edges of the sponges if they have domed in the oven. Place one of the larger sponges on a board and cut it horizontally into 3 even slices. Spread the cut surfaces with buttercream and jam and sandwich them back together. Place this cake on a serving plate, flat side up trimming the base slightly so that it doesn't wobble.

10. Take the second large sponge and cut it vertically into 6 even slices. Spread with buttercream and jam and sandwich the slices back together. Place this cake on top of the first one, flat sides together. Use a palette knife to cover the sponge sphere with an even crumb coat of buttercream.

11. Cut the smaller sponges in half horizontally, spread the cut surfaces with jam and buttercream and sandwich them back together. Spread the flat bottom of one sponge with jam and the other with buttercream and press them together to make the snowman's head. Cover with an even crumb coat of buttercream.

ICE THE CAKE WITH THE MERINGUE FROSTING

12. Make the meringue frosting following the instructions on page 23.

13. Working quickly, as this frosting must be used immediately or it will set, use a palette knife to spread the frosting in an even, generous layer over the snowman's body. Position the head on top of the body and cover it with more frosting. Leave to set for about 2 hours.

ADD THE SNOWMAN'S FEATURES

14. Meanwhile, assemble the snowman's red hat. Brush a little water over the bottom edge of the sugarpaste ring and place it over the larger disc, keeping the cutter in place to give the hat structure. Brush the top edge of the ring with water and press the smaller disc on top. Gently press all the pieces together to stick. Roll the reserved nugget of blue fondant icing to make a long strip and wrap it around the join of the hat, sealing the ends with a little water.

15. Press the black sugarpaste balls into the head for the snowman's eyes and press the nose into his face. Wrap a scarf around his neck and place the hat on top of his head. Press chocolate stick biscuits into the snowman's body for arms and blue sugar-coated chocolate drops down his front for buttons. Dust the cake board with icing sugar and scatter with white chocolate-coated coconut and almond balls to serve.

SECRET CENTRE CHOCOLATE CAKE

SERVES 12–16

Fill the middle of this cake with your child's favourite candies and sweets and decorate the outside with homemade Jazzies or rainbow drops. These are simple to make and the kids will love to help decorate them in an assortment of sprinkles.

FOR THE CHOCOLATE SPONGE

300g unsalted butter, plus extra for greasing

300g caster sugar

100g soft light brown sugar

2 teaspoons vanilla extract

6 medium eggs, lightly beaten

375g plain flour

75g cocoa powder

4 teaspoons baking powder

a pinch of salt

100ml whole milk

125ml boiling water

FOR THE CREAM CHEESE BUTTERCREAM

225g unsalted butter

225g full-fat cream cheese

2 teaspoons vanilla bean paste

600g icing sugar

FOR THE SECRET CENTRE

400g assorted sweets such as sugar-coated chocolate drops and dolly mixture

FOR THE DECORATION

100g dark chocolate, chopped

100g milk chocolate, chopped

100g white chocolate, chopped

sprinkles in various colours

YOU WILL ALSO NEED

3 x 20cm round cake tins

2 x large baking sheets

9cm round cutter

3 x disposable piping bags

MAKE THE CHOCOLATE SPONGE

1. Preheat the oven to 180°C/160°C fan/gas mark 4 and position the shelves as close to the middle as possible, leaving enough space between them for the cakes to rise. Butter the cake tins and line the bases with buttered baking parchment.

2. Make the chocolate sponge mix following the instructions on page 18, up to the end of step 3.

3. Divide the mixture evenly between the prepared tins, spreading it level with a palette knife or the back of a spoon. Bake for 30 minutes until well risen and a skewer inserted into the centre of the sponges comes out clean. Leave to rest in the tins for 3–4 minutes and then carefully turn out onto a wire rack and leave until cold.

MAKE THE BUTTERCREAM AND CHOCOLATE DROPS

4. Cream the butter until really soft and light. Add the cream cheese and vanilla bean paste and mix again until smooth. Gradually add the sifted icing sugar and mix slowly until combined, scraping down the bowl from time to time to ensure the buttercream is evenly mixed. Cover and chill until needed.

5. Line the baking sheets with parchment paper and pop them in the fridge to chill. Melt the dark chocolate in a heatproof bowl set over a pan of barely simmering water, making sure the bottom doesn't touch the water, or in the microwave on a low setting. Stir until smooth and leave to cool slightly, then spoon into the piping bag and snip the end to a fine point. Pipe chocolate button shapes onto the chilled baking sheets in different sizes and cover them with sprinkles. Repeat with the milk and white chocolate and leave all the buttons in a cool place for about 30 minutes to set firm. If it's warm, pop the baking sheets back in the fridge.

ASSEMBLE AND DECORATE THE CAKE

6. Use a large serrated knife to level the tops of 2 of the sponge layers. Stack them, one on top of the other, and use the cutter to stamp out a hole from the middle of both layers, making sure the hole is in exactly the same position in each. Use the sponge shapes you cut out for something else, such as Cake Pops (page 146).

7. Place one of the sponge rings on a cake board or plate and spread the top with a layer of buttercream. Press the second ring on top and spread it with more buttercream. Tip the secret centre sweets into the middle of the hole, filling it to the top. Lay the third, complete sponge layer on top and gently press it down to secure it. Cover the top and sides of the cake with a thin, even crumb coat of buttercream and pop it into the fridge for 30 minutes to set.

8. Use a palette knife to spread the top and sides of the cake with the remaining buttercream. Carefully lift the chocolate drops from the parchment paper using a clean palette knife and arrange them around the sides of the cake. Scatter more sprinkles around the top edge of the cake and serve.

> TO MAKE SURE YOUR CAKE LAYERS ARE EXACTLY THE SAME THICKNESS, WEIGH THE RAW MIXTURE AND DIVIDE IT EVENLY BETWEEN THE PREPARED CAKE TINS.

OMBRÉ RUFFLE CAKE

SERVES 12–16

This cake does require a little patience, a steady hand, some piping skill and an icing turntable, and practice makes perfect! But it really does have the wow factor so it's worth taking the time to master the technique.

FOR THE CHOCOLATE SPONGE

300g unsalted butter, plus extra for greasing

300g caster sugar

100g soft light brown sugar

2 teaspoons vanilla extract

6 eggs, lightly beaten

375g plain flour

80g cocoa powder

4 teaspoons baking powder

a pinch of salt

100ml whole milk

120ml boiling water

4–6 tablespoons raspberry jam

FOR THE VANILLA BUTTERCREAM

400g unsalted butter

800g icing sugar

4 tablespoons milk

2 shades of pink food-colouring paste

YOU WILL ALSO NEED

3 x 18cm round cake tins

disposable piping bags

No. 104 petal/ruffle piping nozzle

icing turntable

fresh flowers, such as ranunculuses, stalks trimmed and wrapped in tin foil

MAKE THE CHOCOLATE SPONGE

1. Preheat the oven to 180°C/160°C fan/gas mark 4 and position the shelves as close to the middle as possible, leaving enough space between them for the cakes to rise. Grease the cake tins and line the bases with discs of buttered baking parchment.

2. Make the chocolate sponge mix following the instructions on page 18, up to the end of step 3.

3. Divide the mixture evenly between the prepared tins, levelling them with a palette knife or the back of a spoon and bake for 30 minutes until well risen and a skewer inserted into the centre of the sponges comes out clean. Leave to rest in the tins for 3–4 minutes and then carefully turn the cakes out onto a wire rack and leave until cold.

ASSEMBLE THE CAKE

4. Make the vanilla buttercream following the instructions on page 22.

5. Lay the sponge layers on the work surface and use a large serrated knife to level the tops. Lay one sponge on a serving plate, spread it with buttercream and top with a layer of jam. Repeat until the cake is assembled, then cover the whole cake with a thin, even crumb coat layer of buttercream, spreading it smoothly with a palette knife. Place the cake on the turntable.

PIPE THE RUFFLES

6. Fit the piping bag with the nozzle and spoon in 3–4 tablespoons of buttercream, chilling the rest. You're going to pipe your first ruffle at the top outside edge of the cake. Imagine the opening of the nozzle is a petal and, holding the fattest end of the petal against the sponge, pipe a ring of ruffles all around the top edge of the cake, turning the turntable with your other hand as you do so. The frosting should sit at a right-angle to the side of the cake.

7. Adjust the angle of your piping hand slightly and pipe a second ring of ruffles on top of the cake, right up against the first one. This should be at roughly a 45-degree angle to the top of the cake. Pipe a couple more ruffles inside this one, towards the centre of the top of the cake, and 2 more rings down the side, directly below the first one. Start each ruffle from the same place each time.

8. Squeeze any leftover icing back into the bowl and tint the whole batch the palest shade of pink using a tiny amount of food-colouring paste on a cocktail stick. Scoop 3–4 tablespoons of icing into a clean piping bag and pipe 2 or 3 rings of ruffles on top of the cake, right up against the white ruffle rings. Pipe more ruffles down the sides of the cake.

9. Squeeze any leftover icing back into the bowl and tint the icing a shade darker. Using a clean piping bag, pipe more ruffle rings around and on top of the cake. The number of rings you pipe and shades you darken the frosting to will depend on the thickness of the ruffles. Keep darkening the buttercream and piping until the cake is completely covered.

10. Carefully place the flowers in the centre of the cake before serving.

SNOW QUEEN

SERVES 12–16

This cake is a dream for most little girls! You don't need any specialist cake tins, just a heatproof mixing bowl or pudding basin and a doll cake pick topper, which are easily available from cake and bake suppliers or online. Although you can pipe elaborate buttercream swirls and ruffles onto the skirt, this Snow Queen would look just as beautiful scattered liberally with hundreds and thousands or sprinkles.

FOR THE VANILLA SPONGE

350g unsalted butter

350g caster sugar

2 teaspoons vanilla extract

6 eggs, lightly beaten

300g plain flour

50g cornflour

4 teaspoons baking powder

a pinch of salt

5 tablespoons milk

8 tablespoons raspberry or apricot jam

FOR THE VANILLA BUTTERCREAM

350g unsalted butter

700g icing sugar, sifted

2 teaspoons vanilla extract

3 tablespoons milk

FOR THE DECORATION

edible silver balls

white mimosa sugar balls

blue food-colouring paste

sugar pearls

75g ready-roll white fondant icing

edible silver glitter

edible sugar diamonds

icing sugar, for dusting

YOU WILL ALSO NEED

1 x 2-litre heatproof bowl

1 x 20cm round cake tin

several disposable piping bags

medium open star nozzle

no. 104 petal/ruffle piping nozzle

princess doll cake pick topper

MAKE THE VANILLA SPONGE

1. Preheat the oven to 180°C/160°C fan/gas mark 4 and position the shelves as close to the middle as possible, leaving enough space between them for the cakes to rise. Grease the bowl and cake tin and line the bases with buttered baking parchment.

2. Make the vanilla sponge mix following the instructions on page 17, up to the end of step 3.

3. Spoon the cake mix into the prepared bowl, filling it two-thirds full. Spread the remaining mixture into the cake tin. Spread both level with a palette knife or the back of a spoon. Bake the sponge in the tin for about 20 minutes and the sponge in the bowl for about 40–45 minutes, until golden, well risen and a skewer inserted into the centre of the sponges comes out clean. Leave to rest for 3–4 minutes and then carefully turn out onto a wire rack and leave until cold.

ASSEMBLE THE CAKE

4. Make the buttercream following the instructions on page 22.

5. Use a large serrated knife to level the flat edge of the bowl sponge if necessary and then place it on a chopping board. Cut into 3 even horizontal slices and spread the cut sides with thin layers of jam and buttercream. Sandwich the slices back together.

6. Place the flat cake on a serving plate and spread the top with a little jam. Top it with the bowl cake and gently press the cakes together. Use a palette knife to cover the whole cake with a thin crumb coat layer of buttercream and then carefully place alternate edible silver balls and mimosa sugar balls all around the bottom edge of the cake.

PIPE THE SKIRT

7. Fit one of the piping bags with the medium star nozzle and fill it with 4–5 tablespoons of vanilla buttercream. Pipe rosettes around the base of the cake, leaving the silver and mimosa balls just visible. Pipe another row of rosettes above this so that they are only just overlapping the row below.

8. Squeeze any excess buttercream back into the bowl, mix to combine and scoop 3 tablespoons into a small bowl to use later. Tint the remaining buttercream a pale shade of blue using a tiny dot of food-colouring paste. Spoon 3 tablespoons into a clean piping bag fitted with the star nozzle and pipe a row of pale blue rosettes above the white ones. Squeeze the excess buttercream back into the bowl, mix to combine and scoop out 2 tablespoons into a small bowl. Set aside.

9. Tint the remaining buttercream a darker shade of blue and use it to pipe a final row of rosettes.

10. Fit a clean piping bag with the ruffle nozzle and fill it with the reserved white vanilla buttercream. Following the method on page 58, pipe 4–5 ruffle rings above the top ring of rosettes. Next pipe 4–5 rings of pale blue ruffles, followed by rings of dark blue ruffles. Press sugar pearls in between each buttercream rosette all over the skirt of the snow queen.

DRESS THE QUEEN AND FINISH THE CAKE

11. Roll out the fondant icing on a lightly dusted work surface to no more than 2mm thick. Shape a fondant bodice and press it into position on your doll, trimming off any excess. Lightly brush the bodice with water and coat completely with sprinkled edible glitter. Use a dry brush to remove any stray glitter.

12. Press the doll into the middle of the cake and position edible sugar diamonds around her waist. Finally, sprinkle edible glitter over the skirt and serve.

CHANGE THE COLOURS OF THE BUTTERCREAM AND SPRINKLES TO MATCH THE THEME OF YOUR PARTY.

RAINBOW

SERVES 16–20

This cake just makes you smile and feel happy! It really is worth having candy floss for clouds to complete the decoration – candy floss is available ready made in tubs online, or from party supply shops. Candy floss machines are also relatively inexpensive and great fun to use.

FOR THE VANILLA SPONGE

350g unsalted butter

350g caster sugar

2 teaspoons vanilla extract

6 eggs, lightly beaten

300g plain flour

50g cornflour

4 teaspoons baking powder

a pinch of salt

5 tablespoons milk

200g raspberry or apricot jam

FOR THE VANILLA BUTTERCREAM

400g unsalted butter

800g icing sugar, sifted

2 teaspoons vanilla bean paste or extract

4 tablespoons milk

FOR THE DECORATION

rainbow sprinkles

red, orange, yellow, green, blue, indigo and violet food-colouring pastes

40 milk chocolate-coated stick biscuits

gold foil-covered chocolate coins

candy floss, marshmallows or fluffy cream

YOU WILL ALSO NEED

1 x 30cm round cake tin

11–12cm plain round cutter

disposable piping bags

small–medium star nozzles

MAKE THE VANILLA SPONGE

1. Preheat the oven to 180°C/160°C fan/gas mark 4. Grease the cake tin and line the base with a disc of buttered baking parchment.

2. Make the vanilla sponge mix following the instructions on page 17, up to the end of step 3.

3. Scoop the cake mix into the prepared tin and spread it level with a palette knife or the back of a spoon. Bake for 35–40 minutes, until well risen, golden brown and a skewer inserted into the centre of the cake comes out clean. Leave to rest in the tin for 4–5 minutes and then carefully turn out onto a wire rack and leave until cold.

ASSEMBLE THE CAKE

4. Make the vanilla buttercream following the instructions on page 22. Cover and set aside until needed.

5. Place the cake on the work surface and use a large serrated knife to cut it in half vertically so that you have 2 even semicircles. Trim both layers to level the tops and place one on top of the other. Use the cutter to cut out a smaller semicircle from the middle of the straight edge to make a rainbow shape. Wrap the trimmings in cling film and set aside.

6. Unstack the cakes, spread the bottom layer with jam and buttercream and replace the top layer. Cover the top and sides of the cake with a layer of jam and chill for 30 minutes.

DECORATE THE RAINBOW

7. Use a palette knife to cover the top rounded edge, short bottom edges and the edge under the rainbow arc with buttercream, spreading it evenly and smoothly with a palette knife. Chill for a further 30 minutes and then press sprinkles all over the buttercream in an even layer. Carefully transfer the cake to a serving plate or board.

8. Spoon 4 tablespoons of buttercream into a small bowl, cover and set aside. Scoop another 4 tablespoons of buttercream into a small bowl and tint it red using food-colouring paste. Mix until evenly coloured and use it to fill a piping bag fitted with a medium star nozzle. Pipe rosettes of red buttercream all along the top edge of the rainbow.

9. Tint another 4 tablespoons of buttercream orange and pipe a second row of rosettes below the first one. Repeat until you have a rainbow of red, orange, yellow, green, blue, indigo and violet rosettes, in that order, using ever-decreasing amounts of buttercream for each band of colour.

MAKE A POT OF GOLD AND FLUFFY CLOUDS

10. Unwrap the trimmed cake pieces. Spread the flat edges with jam and sandwich them together to make a circle. Cover the top and sides with the reserved buttercream. Position the small cake on the board at one end of the rainbow.

11. Trim the chocolate stick biscuits so that they are about 3cm taller than the small sponge and press them into the buttercream all around the sides of the pot. Fill the pot with the gold coins.

12. Just before serving, make a cloud of candy floss to sit at the other end of the rainbow. If you haven't got candy floss you could use a pile of marshmallows or fluffy cream to make a cloud instead.

JEWELLED CROWN

SERVES 12

Decorate the shortbread crown biscuits as elaborately as you like, or dare, for this cake and assemble it shortly before serving.

FOR THE VANILLA SPONGE

250g unsalted butter
250g caster sugar
4 eggs, lightly beaten
2 teaspoons vanilla extract
200g plain flour
50g cornflour
3 teaspoons baking powder
a pinch of salt
4 tablespoons milk
2–3 tablespoons raspberry jam

FOR THE SHORTBREAD BISCUITS

225g unsalted butter
150g icing sugar
1 egg, lightly beaten
grated zest of ½ unwaxed lemon
1 teaspoon vanilla bean paste
350g plain flour, plus extra for dusting
½ teaspoon baking powder
a pinch of salt

FOR THE VANILLA BUTTERCREAM

250g unsalted butter
500g icing sugar
2 teaspoons vanilla extract
3 tablespoons milk

FOR THE DECORATION

clear fruit-flavoured boiled sweets
200g royal icing sugar
jelly diamonds
silver and gold sugar balls
sugar pearls
red sanding sugar

YOU WILL ALSO NEED

3 x 18cm round cake tins
2 x baking sheets
Crown template, page 14
disposable piping bag
fake fur rope or ribbon

MAKE THE VANILLA SPONGE

1. Preheat the oven to 180°C/160°C fan/gas mark 4 and position the shelves as close to the middle as possible, leaving enough space between them for the cakes to rise. Grease the cake tins and line the bases with discs of buttered baking parchment.

2. Make the vanilla sponge mix following the instructions on page 17, up to the end of step 3.

3. Divide the cake mix evenly between the prepared tins, spreading it level with a palette knife or the back of a spoon. Bake for 20 minutes until golden, well risen and a skewer inserted into the centre of the cakes comes out clean. Leave to rest in the tins for 3–4 minutes and then carefully turn out onto a wire rack and leave until cold.

MAKE AND DECORATE THE BISCUITS

4. Make the shortbread mix following the instructions on page 20 and chill for 2 hours. Line the baking sheets with baking parchment.

5. Roll out the chilled dough on a lightly floured work surface to about 2mm thick. Use the template on page 14 to cut out 9–10 crown shapes (you will only need 8 for the cake, but make extras in case of accidents). Arrange on the prepared baking sheets and chill for 15 minutes.

6. Bake the chilled biscuits for 10 minutes, until firm and only just starting to colour, then remove from the oven and place 1 boiled sweet in the hole at the top of each biscuit and continue to cook for a further 2 minutes, until the shortbread is golden and the boiled sweet jewel has melted and filled the hole. Remove from the oven and leave to cool on the baking sheet.

7. Make the royal icing following the instructions on page 21. Use dots of icing to stick jelly diamonds, sugar balls and pearls to the biscuits and then set aside for about 2 hours to set firm.

ASSEMBLE THE CAKE

8. Make the vanilla buttercream following the instructions on page 22.

9. Place the cake layers on the work surface and use a large serrated knife to level the tops. Place one layer on the serving plate and spread it with a tablespoon of jam. Spread the underside of the second layer with buttercream and sandwich the two together. Repeat with the third layer. Use a palette knife to cover the whole cake with buttercream, swirling the cream towards the centre on the top to resemble velvet folds, and sprinkle the top liberally with sanding sugar.

10. Just before serving, position the crown biscuits around the sides of the cake, securing with a little jam or buttercream and tie a piece of fake fur or a ribbon around the base.

MAKE JEWELLED BISCUITS FROM THE LEFTOVER SHORTBREAD DOUGH. STAMP OUT CIRCLES AND THEN SMALLER CIRCLES FROM THE MIDDLES. FILL WITH ROUGHLY CHOPPED BOILED SWEETS AND BAKE AS ABOVE.

CHECKERBOARD LAYER CAKE

SERVES 12–16

This cake is a showstopper with added wow factor! Take your time both when measuring the batter evenly between the cake tins and when you cut out the sponge circles to make sure you get a perfect, professional finish. Freeze-dried fruit powders are available in specialist grocers or online.

FOR THE VANILLA SPONGE (2 BATCHES)

2 x 175g unsalted butter
2 x 175g caster sugar
2 x 1 teaspoon vanilla extract
2 x 3 large eggs, lightly beaten
2 x 150g plain flour
2 x 25g cornflour
2 x 2 teaspoons baking powder
2 x a pinch of salt
2 x 2 tablespoons milk
pink food-colouring paste
200g seedless raspberry or apricot jam

FOR THE MERINGUE BUTTERCREAM

250g caster sugar
4 egg whites
1 teaspoon vanilla extract
a pinch of salt
325g unsalted butter
2 tablespoons freeze-dried plum or raspberry powder

FOR THE DECORATION

confetti sprinkles

YOU WILL ALSO NEED

2 x 18cm round cake tins
plain round cutters – 4cm, 8cm and 12cm
disposable piping bag
open star nozzle

MAKE THE VANILLA SPONGES

1. Preheat the oven to 180°C/160°C fan/gas mark 4 and position the shelves as close to the middle as possible, leaving enough space between them for the cakes to rise. Grease the cake tins and line the bases with discs of buttered baking parchment.

2. You're going to make 2 batches of vanilla sponge, 1 plain and 1 pink. Use 1 batch of ingredients to make the first mixture following the instructions on page 17, up to the end of step 3, leaving out the food colouring. Weigh the mixture and divide it equally between the prepared tins, spreading it level with a palette knife or the back of a spoon. Bake for 20 minutes until golden, well risen and a skewer inserted into the centres comes out clean. Leave to rest in the tins for 3–4 minutes and then carefully turn out onto wire racks. Wash, dry and re-line the tins.

the sponge, again leaving the cut section in place. Repeat with the 4cm cutter. You should now have 1 small disc and 3 larger rings. Repeat for all 4 sponges, leaving them all intact.

7. Start with 1 pink and 1 plain sponge layer. Take the largest ring from the pink sponge and position it on a serving plate. Using a palette knife, spread the inside of the ring with jam. Take the 12cm plain ring and sit it inside the first ring. Spread the inside with jam and place the 8cm pink circle inside. Brush with jam and place the small plain disc in the middle so that you have a single layer of alternating pink and plain sponge rings.

8. Pipe an even layer of buttercream across the top of the whole layer and use a palette knife to spread it level. Repeat with the second set of sponge rings, starting with the largest plain ring, and carefully place on top of the first layer. Cover with buttercream.

9. Repeat steps 7 and 8 for the remaining sponge layers. You should now have 4 alternating layers of plain and pink sponge.

10. Cover the top and sides of the cake with buttercream, spreading it smoothly using a palette knife. Scatter confetti sprinkles around the top edge and up the sides of the cake and serve.

3. Make a second batch of vanilla sponge, adding pink food-colouring paste to the mixture with a cocktail stick once all the other ingredients have been incorporated. Mix well so that the colour is even throughout. Divide the mixture evenly between the tins and bake as above. Set aside until completely cold.

ASSEMBLE THE CAKE

4. Make the meringue buttercream following the instructions on page 23. Add the freeze-dried fruit powder at the end and whisk to combine.

5. Lay the 4 sponges on the work surface and use a large serrated knife to level the tops.

6. Take the 12cm cutter and position it in the centre of one of the sponges. Cut through the sponge to the base, but don't remove the cut middle. Take the 8cm cutter, position it in the centre of the same sponge layer and cut through

IF YOU CAN'T FIND FREEZE-DRIED FRUIT POWDER, BUY FREEZE-DRIED RASPBERRIES AND STRAWBERRIES AND WHIZZ SMALL PIECES IN A FOOD-PROCESSOR.

DOLL'S HOUSE

SERVES 12

This is a gingerbread house for those who don't want the pressure of making a three-dimensional construction! The sponge is hidden inside the gingerbread walls and is constructed in exactly the same way as the Dog Kennel on page 42.

FOR THE VANILLA SPONGE

350g unsalted butter

350g caster sugar

2 teaspoons vanilla extract

6 eggs, lightly beaten

300g plain flour

50g cornflour

4 teaspoons baking powder

4 tablespoons milk

6–8 tablespoons raspberry or apricot jam

FOR THE GINGERBREAD

3 tablespoons golden syrup

1 tablespoon treacle

3 egg yolks

400g plain flour, plus extra for dusting

3 teaspoons ground ginger

2 teaspoons ground cinnamon

1 teaspoon mixed spice

1 teaspoon baking powder

a large pinch of salt

200g unsalted butter, chilled and diced

100g light muscovado sugar

50g caster sugar

FOR THE VANILLA BUTTERCREAM

250g unsalted butter

500g icing sugar

2 teaspoons vanilla extract

2 tablespoons milk

FOR THE DECORATION

500g royal icing sugar

pink and blue food-colouring pastes

200g chocolate buttons

edible sugar flowers

YOU WILL ALSO NEED

2 x 20cm square cake tins

baking sheets

Doll's House template, page 14

3–4 disposable piping bags

MAKE THE VANILLA SPONGE

1. Preheat the oven to 180°C/160°C fan/gas mark 4 and position the shelves as close to the middle as possible, leaving enough space between them for the cakes to rise. Grease the cake tins and line the bases with squares of buttered baking parchment.

2. Make the vanilla sponge mix following the instructions on page 17, up to the end of step 3.

3. Divide the cake mix between the prepared tins and spread them level using a palette knife or the back of a spoon. Bake for 30–35 minutes until golden brown, well risen and a skewer inserted into the centre of the sponges comes out clean. Leave to cool in the tins for 5 minutes and then turn out onto a wire rack and leave until cold before wrapping in cling film.

MAKE THE GINGERBREAD WALLS

4. Use a warmed measuring spoon to measure the golden syrup and treacle into a small bowl. Add the egg yolks and mix well to combine.

5. Sieve the flour, ginger, cinnamon, mixed spice, baking powder and salt into a large mixing bowl or the bowl of a stand mixer. Add the butter and rub it in either using your fingers or by using the paddle attachment. When there are no flecks of butter visible add the light muscovado and caster sugars and mix again to combine.

6. Make a well in the middle of the dry mixture and add the eggy syrup mixture and mix until the dough starts to come together into clumps. Use your hands to gently knead the dough until smooth, but try not to overwork it or you will stretch the gluten strands in the flour, resulting in dough that is tough and may shrink and misshape during cooking. Flatten the dough into a disc, weigh it and divide it in half. Wrap it in cling film and chill for 2 hours. Line a baking sheet with baking parchment.

7. Take 1 portion of dough and cut it into 2 pieces, one slightly larger than the other. Roll out the larger piece on a lightly dusted work surface to a neat square. Use the template on page 14 as a guide to cut out the shape for the side of the house. Carefully slide onto the prepared baking sheet. Use the smaller piece of dough to cut out a 20 x 20cm square for the front of the house. Repeat with the second portion of dough so that you have 2 house fronts and 2 sides. Chill for 20 minutes. Preheat the oven to 180°C/160°C fan/gas mark 4.

8. Bake the gingerbread for about 15 minutes, until firm and just starting to darken at the edges. Remove from the oven and leave to cool on the baking sheets.

HEAT A MEASURING SPOON IN A MUG OF BOILING WATER FOR 1 MINUTE TO MAKE IT EASIER AND LESS MESSY TO MEASURE GOLDEN SYRUP AND TREACLE.

DECORATE THE GINGERBREAD WALLS

9. Prepare the royal icing following the instructions on page 21, until it holds a firm ribbon trail when the whisk is lifted from the bowl. Spoon 3–4 tablespoons into a disposable piping bag, twist the end to seal and snip the point into a fine nozzle. Cover the remaining icing with cling film to prevent it drying out.

10. Pipe a border around the edge of each gingerbread section and decorate with windows, doors and roof tiles.

11. Spoon 2 tablespoons of royal icing into a small bowl and colour it a very pale blue using a tiny dot of food-colouring paste. Spoon into a disposable piping bag, snip the end to a point and fill the door section.

12. Tint another 2 tablespoons of the icing pink and pipe curtains for each window. Leave to dry for at least 30 minutes.

ASSEMBLE THE HOUSE

13. Make the vanilla buttercream following the instructions on page 22.

14. Using the diagram on page 15 as a guide to help you, use a large serrated knife to cut the sponge cakes into rectangles measuring 20 × 14cm, then cut these in half horizontally to make 4 even slices. Place 1 slice on a serving plate and spread the top with jam. Top with a second slice and spread with buttercream. Repeat, alternating the jam with the buttercream.

15. Take one of the remaining small sections of sponge and cut it in half diagonally to make two 20cm-long triangular wedges. Sit the 2 triangles side by side to make a pitched roof. Spread a little jam along the long side to stick them together and place on top of the cake stack. You will not need the last piece of cake for this recipe.

16. Cover the sides and top of the cake in buttercream, spreading it smoothly and evenly with a palette knife. Press chocolate drops onto the sponge roof in an overlapping pattern to resemble roof tiles.

17. Use a dab of extra buttercream to stick the gingerbread walls to the sides of the cake and decorate the front of the house with icing flowers. You can also tint a little of the royal icing to pipe your house number, or the age of the child, onto the front door.

MAD HATTER'S CAKE

Alice in Wonderland and the Mad Hatter's tea party are perennial favourite party themes, and this cake is a perfect centrepiece. It is made with alternate layers of rich chocolate and light vanilla sponge.

FOR THE CHOCOLATE SPONGE

300g unsalted butter, plus extra for greasing

300g caster sugar

100g soft light brown sugar

2 teaspoons vanilla extract

6 eggs, lightly beaten

375g plain flour

80g cocoa powder

4 teaspoons baking powder

a pinch of salt

100ml milk

120ml boiling water

400g raspberry jam

FOR THE VANILLA SPONGE

200g unsalted butter

200g caster sugar

2 teaspoons vanilla extract

3 eggs, lightly beaten

175g plain flour

25g cornflour

2½ teaspoons baking powder

a pinch of salt

3 tablespoons milk

FOR THE VANILLA BUTTERCREAM

250g unsalted butter

500g icing sugar

3–4 tablespoons milk

2 teaspoons vanilla extract

FOR THE DECORATION

1.5kg ready-roll white fondant icing

blue and green food-colouring pastes

icing sugar, for dusting

YOU WILL ALSO NEED

2 x 18cm round cake tins

1 x 20cm round cake tin

string, for measuring

MAKE THE CHOCOLATE SPONGE

1. Preheat the oven to 180°C/160°C fan/gas mark 4 and position the shelves as close to the middle as possible, leaving enough space between them for the cakes to rise. Grease the cake tins and line the bases with discs of buttered baking parchment.

2. Make the chocolate sponge mix following the instructions on page 18, up to the end of step 3.

3. Divide the cake mix evenly between the 3 prepared tins and spread it level with a palette knife or the back of a spoon. Bake for 30 minutes until well risen and a skewer inserted into the centre of the sponges comes out clean. Leave to rest in the tins for 3–4 minutes and then carefully turn out onto a wire rack and leave until cold. Clean, grease and reline one of the 18cm tins and the 20cm tin.

MAKE THE VANILLA SPONGE

4. Make the vanilla sponge mix following the instructions on page 17, up to the end of step 3.

5. Divide the cake mix between the 2 prepared tins. Bake for 25–30 minutes or until golden brown, well risen and a skewer inserted into the centre of the sponges comes out clean. Leave to rest in the tins for 3–4 minutes and then carefully turn out onto a wire rack and leave until cold.

ASSEMBLE THE CAKE

6. Make the vanilla buttercream following the instructions on page 22.

7. Lay all the sponges on the work surface and use a large serrated knife to level the tops. Lay one of the smaller chocolate sponges on a chopping board and spread it with jam. Spread the underside of the small vanilla sponge with buttercream and sandwich the two together. Repeat with the small chocolate layer and then the 2 large layers. You should end up with one big cake with 5 layers in alternate flavours, the smaller ones on the bottom and the larger ones on top.

8. Using the large knife, slice the edges downwards from just below the bottom of the top layer and taper in to create a hat shape. Brush away any crumbs and use the offcuts for something else. Use a palette knife to spread the cake with a smooth crumb coat layer of buttercream, filling any gaps and holes as you do so.

DECORATE THE HAT

9. Break off 150g of the fondant icing and tint it green using food-colouring paste, cover with cling film and set aside.

10. Tint the remaining fondant pale blue. Slice off 200g and cover the remainder with cling film. Roll out the 200g piece on a lightly dusted work surface and use the base of the 20cm cake tin to cut it to a neat circle, reserving any trimmings. Lay this disc on top of the cake and press it smoothly into place with your hands.

11. Use a length of string to measure the height of the cake and the circumference at the widest part. Knead the trimmings back into the reserved blue fondant and roll out 600g to a neat rectangle 1cm taller than the cake and a little wider than its circumference. Trim the bottom edge and, starting at one of the shorter edges, roll up the rectangle neatly as if you were rolling up a carpet.

12. Decide what will be the back of your cake and brush a 1cm line of jam from the top to the bottom. Lightly press the long edge of the rolled fondant into the jam and carefully unroll it around the cake with the neatened edge at the bottom. When you have unrolled all the icing, seal the edges using a little water to stick it together. Use a pair of scissors to neatly trim any excess and then smooth the icing into place with the palms of your hands. Trim any excess from the top and gently pinch together the top of the hat and the sides to seal. Use the blunt end of a wooden skewer to make little 'stitch' marks around the top edge of the hat.

13. Knead any trimmings back into the remaining blue fondant and roll it out to a neat 23cm disc. Carefully roll this up, trying not to stretch it out of shape, and unroll it onto a serving plate. Use a cake lifter or 2 fish slices to position the cake in the middle of the disc. Your hat is nearly complete!

14. Cut off a quarter of the green fondant and set it aside. Roll out the large piece to a neat 3cm strip that's the same length as the circumference of the bottom of the hat. Lightly brush the base of the hat with water, roll up the green strip and, starting at the back of the hat, unroll it neatly around it.

15. Roll out the remaining green fondant to a strip the same width and thickness as the hat band. Trim off a 10cm piece from one end. Fold the edges of the longer piece back on themselves to make a bow shape and wrap the shorter piece around the middle, attaching it with a little water. Brush the back of the bow with water and position it on the hat band. Use the skewer to create stitch marks along the length of the hat band and around the bow. Leave for 2 hours to dry completely before serving.

TO TINT FONDANT, ADD TINY DOTS OF COLOUR USING A COCKTAIL STICK OR SKEWER AND KNEAD UNTIL THE FONDANT IS SMOOTH AND EVEN BEFORE ADDING MORE COLOUR.

FORTRESS

SERVES 24–30

What child (or grown-up) doesn't love a fortress complete with toy soldiers, knights and dragons? And when that fortress is made from chocolate cake, coated in buttercream, decorated with chocolate biscuits, sweets and topped with ice-cream cone turrets... This cake is large enough to feed a small army.

FOR THE LARGE SPONGES

300g unsalted butter, plus extra for greasing

300g caster sugar

100g soft light brown sugar

2 teaspoons vanilla extract

6 eggs, lightly beaten

375g plain flour

80g cocoa powder

4 teaspoons baking powder

a pinch of salt

100ml whole milk

120ml boiling water

FOR THE SMALL SPONGES

200g unsalted butter

200g caster sugar

60g soft light brown sugar

1 teaspoon vanilla extract

4 eggs, lightly beaten

250g plain flour

50g cocoa powder

3 teaspoons baking powder

4 tablespoons whole milk

6 tablespoons boiling water

FOR THE VANILLA BUTTERCREAM

250g unsalted butter

400g icing sugar, sifted

2 teaspoons vanilla extract

3–4 tablespoons milk

FOR THE CHOCOLATE BUTTERCREAM

350g unsalted butter

700g icing sugar, sifted

100g cocoa powder, sifted

4 tablespoons milk

2 tablespoons golden syrup

2 teaspoons vanilla extract

FOR THE DECORATION

2 x 365g jumbo chocolate Swiss rolls

2 x packets chocolate-coated finger biscuits

a few white chocolate-coated finger biscuits

milk chocolate-coated stick biscuits

chocolate buttons

chocolate-coated crunchy almond butter sweets

chocolate-coated curly caramel bars

200g dark chocolate, melted

4 x waffle ice-cream cones

chocolate sprinkles

YOU WILL ALSO NEED

2 x 20cm square cake tins

2 x 15cm square cake tins

8cm round cutter

paper flags

miniature knights and dragons, optional

MAKE THE SPONGES

1. Preheat the oven to 180°C/160°C fan/gas mark 4 and position the shelves as close to the middle as possible, leaving enough space between them for the cakes to rise. Grease the cake tins and line the bases with buttered baking parchment.

2. Make the chocolate sponge mix for the large cakes following the instructions on page 18, up to the end of step 3.

3. Divide the cake mix evenly between the prepared 20cm tins and spread it level with a palette knife or the back of a spoon. Bake for 30–35 minutes until well risen and a skewer inserted into the middle of the cakes comes out clean. Leave to rest in the tins for 3–4 minutes and then carefully turn out onto a wire rack and leave until cold.

4. Repeat steps 2 and 3 to make the smaller sponge layers using the 15cm tins.

ASSEMBLE THE CAKE

5. Make the vanilla buttercream following the instructions on page 22.

6. Lay the large sponge layers on the work surface and use a large serrated knife to level the tops, reserving the trimmings. Slice each layer in half horizontally and spread the bottom layers with vanilla buttercream. Sandwich with the top layers and spread one with more buttercream, then stack the 4 layers to make one big cake.

7. Repeat step 6 with the small sponge layers and position them on top of the large layers.

8. Use the round cutter to cut away the corners of the large sponge layers – this is where the towers will be positioned.

9. Make the chocolate buttercream following the instructions on page 23.

10. Cut each Swiss roll in half widthways and place one half at each corner of the fortress. Use a palette knife to cover the whole cake, including the turrets, with chocolate buttercream.

DECORATE THE FORTRESS

11. Press 3 or 4 white chocolate fingers into the buttercream at the centre of the bottom storey of the fortress to make a door. Press milk-chocolate fingers around the rest of the walls, except for the towers, and lay chocolate-coated stick biscuits on the step between the two storeys to cover the buttercream.

12. Position chocolate buttons on the towers to resemble windows, create battlements using the crunchy almond butter sweets and a drawbridge using curly caramel bars.

13. Melt the chocolate in a bowl set over barely simmering water, making sure the bottom of the bowl doesn't touch the water, or in the microwave on a low setting. Use it to cover the ice-cream cones and, when almost set, roll the cones in the sprinkles. Leave to set before positioning a cone upside down on each tower.

14. Stick a flag into each tower, scatter the crumbled sponge trimmings around the base, decorate with knights and dragons, if using, and serve.

TURN THIS CAKE INTO A FAIRY CASTLE BY COATING IT IN VANILLA BUTTERCREAM, WHITE CHOCOLATE-COATED FINGER BISCUITS AND PRETTY SWEETS.

SPACE ROCKET

SERVES 16

This cake is guaranteed to elicit squeals of delight! The cakes can be baked and iced in advance and assembled on the day of the party. Look out for food-safe sparklers for the rocket launchers and stand back for lift off!

FOR THE VANILLA SPONGE

350g unsalted butter, plus extra for greasing

350g caster sugar

2 teaspoons vanilla extract

6 eggs, lightly beaten

300g plain flour

50g cornflour

4 teaspoons baking powder

a pinch of salt

5 tablespoons milk

400g raspberry or smooth apricot seedless jam

FOR THE SHORTBREAD BISCUITS

125g unsalted butter

75g icing sugar

1 egg yolk

1 teaspoon vanilla bean paste

175g plain flour, plus extra for dusting

¼ teaspoon baking powder

a pinch of salt

FOR THE VANILLA BUTTERCREAM

250g unsalted butter

500g icing sugar, sifted

2 teaspoons vanilla extract

2 tablespoons milk

FOR THE DECORATION

1kg ready-roll white fondant icing

400g red fondant icing or sugarpaste

150g royal icing sugar, plus extra for rolling

edible silver balls

YOU WILL ALSO NEED

3 x 15cm round cake tins

1 x 10cm round cake tin

1 x dariole mould or muffin tin

Rocket fin template, page 14

baking sheet

12 cardboard ovenproof and food-safe cake pop sticks

string, for measuring

disposable piping bag

food-safe sparklers

MAKE THE VANILLA SPONGE

1. Preheat the oven to 180°C/160°C fan/gas mark 4 and position the shelves as close to the middle as possible, leaving enough space between them for the cakes to rise. Grease the cake tins and dariole mould or muffin tin and line the tins with discs of buttered baking parchment.

2. Make the vanilla sponge mix following the instructions on page 17, up to the end of step 3.

POSITION THE SMALLER CAKES, WHICH COOK FASTER, AT THE FRONT OF THE OVEN TO MAKE IT EASY TO REMOVE THEM WITHOUT MOVING THE LARGER CAKES.

3. Spoon the cake mix into the prepared tins so that they are half full and spread level with a palette knife or the back of a spoon. Bake for 15 minutes for the smallest sponge and 25 minutes for the larger ones, until golden brown, well risen and a skewer inserted into the centre of the sponges comes out clean. Leave to cool in the tins for 5 minutes and then turn out onto a wire rack and leave until completely cold, then wrap in cling film.

MAKE THE SHORTBREAD FINS

4. Meanwhile, make the shortbread mix following the instructions on page 20 and chill. Line a baking sheet with baking parchment.

5. Roll out the chilled dough on a lightly dusted work surface to 2–3mm thick. Use the template on page 14 to cut out 6 fins, re-rolling any scraps, and arrange them spaced well apart on the prepared baking sheet. You will only need 4 fins for the cake but it's wise to have spares in case of emergencies.

6. Press a lolly or cake pop stick horizontally across one of the fins, about 3cm below the triangular top point. Press a second stick about 3cm below the first one. The sticks should reach almost all the way across the width of the fin and stick out by about 5cm on the long side. Very lightly brush a drop of water over the embedded lolly stick and press a little of the leftover dough over the top to seal the stick in place. Repeat with the remaining fins. Chill for 20 minutes.

7. Bake the biscuits for 12–15 minutes until firm and light brown. Leave to cool on the baking sheet.

ASSEMBLE THE CAKES

8. Make the vanilla buttercream following the instructions on page 22.

9. Lay the sponges on the work surface and use a large serrated knife to level the tops. Spread the top of the first 15cm layer with a tablespoon of jam and the underside of the next one with buttercream. Sandwich the two together and spread the top with another tablespoon of jam. Spread the underside of the final 15cm layer with buttercream and place it on top.

10. Slice the 10cm cake in half horizontally. Spread the bottom half with jam and buttercream and sandwich the layers back together.

11. Use a palette knife to spread the remaining buttercream in a smooth, even layer over the top and sides of the large cake stack, the 10cm cake and the small cake.

ICE THE CAKES

12. Divide the white fondant into 2 and wrap one half in cling film. Cut 150g from the other half and roll it out on a lightly dusted work surface to a neat 15cm disc – use the base of the cake tin as a guide. Place on top of the large cake and smooth into place with your hands.

13. Use a piece of string to measure the height and circumference of the large cake and roll the 350g fondant piece to a neat rectangle with the same measurements. Trim the top and bottom edges to neaten them and, starting at a short edge, roll it up like a carpet. Starting at the back of the cake, holding the fondant in line with the bottom edge, unroll the icing around the sides of the cake, sealing the join with a little water. Smooth into place with your hands.

14. Use two-thirds of the remaining white fondant to cover the 10cm cake in the same way. Roll the remaining fondant into a disc and cover the smallest cake, trimming off any excess and smoothing the icing into place with your hands. Leave all the cakes for 30 minutes before stacking them on a cake stand, with the icing seams lined up at the back.

DECORATE THE ROCKET

15. Prepare the royal icing following the instructions on page 21, until you have a smooth paste that holds a firm ribbon trail when the whisk is lifted from the bowl. Spoon into a disposable piping bag, twist the end to seal and snip the point to a fine nozzle.

16. Pipe a thin line of icing around the top edge of the largest cake, where the fondant icing joins, and press silver balls into the icing in a neat line. Pipe a second line where the cakes meet and decorate with silver balls, as before. Pipe a line of icing around the join where the 2 smaller cakes meet and decorate with silver balls.

17. Roll out half the red icing or sugarpaste between 2 clean sheets of baking parchment to 1–2mm thick. Remove the top sheet of parchment and cut the icing into neat 2cm squares. Brush one side of each square with a tiny dab of water and arrange them around the base of the bottom cake, 2cm apart. Arrange another 2 rows above the first one to make a checkerboard pattern.

18. Break off another 75g of the red icing and shape it into a cone. Position this on top of the rocket and pipe a line of royal icing around the bottom edge. Press silver balls into the icing to conceal the join.

19. Roll the remaining red icing out between clean sheets of parchment to 1mm thick and use the template to cut out 12 fin shapes. Cover with cling film until needed.

20. Lay the biscuit fins on the work surface with the lolly sticks underneath. Brush lightly with jam and carefully stick a red fondant fin onto each biscuit. Leave to dry for 10 minutes and then flip them over and cover the backs. Leave to dry for a further 10–15 minutes.

21. When you are ready to serve the cake, press 4 fins into the side of the biggest cake, at even intervals. Push food-safe sparklers into the bottom of the cake, light the boosters and step back for lift off!

BUCKET & SPADE

SERVES 16

Perfect for a beach-themed party, this cake is decorated with a selection of beautiful iced shells tucked in amongst the sandcrumbs – with the odd crab lurking and ready to nip toes. Look online at baking supply websites for an assortment of biscuit cutters.

FOR THE VANILLA SPONGE

350g unsalted butter

350g caster sugar

2 teaspoons vanilla extract

6 eggs, lightly beaten

300g plain flour

50g cornflour

4 teaspoons baking powder

a pinch of salt

5 tablespoons milk

FOR THE SHORTBREAD BISCUITS

225g unsalted butter

150g icing sugar

1 egg, lightly beaten

grated zest of ½ unwaxed lemon

1 teaspoon vanilla bean paste

350g plain flour, plus extra for dusting

½ teaspoon baking powder

a pinch of salt

FOR THE VANILLA BUTTERCREAM

250g unsalted butter

500g icing sugar

2 teaspoons vanilla extract

3 tablespoons milk

8 tablespoons seedless raspberry jam

FOR THE DECORATION

500g royal icing sugar, plus extra for dusting

assorted food-colouring pastes, including red and blue

edible sugar pearls, optional

1kg white ready-roll fondant icing

400g digestive biscuits, crushed

YOU WILL ALSO NEED

2 x 18cm round cake tins

2 x 15cm round cake tins

Spade template, page 14

seaside biscuit cutters, such as seashells, crabs and starfish

baking sheet

disposable piping bags

MAKE THE VANILLA SPONGE

1. Preheat the oven to 180°C/160°C fan/gas mark 4 and position the shelves as close to the middle as possible, leaving enough space between them for the cakes to rise. Grease the cake tins and line the bases with discs of buttered baking parchment.

2. Make the vanilla sponge mix following the instructions on page 17 up to the end of step 3.

3. Divide the cake mix evenly between the prepared tins, levelling the tops with a palette knife or the back of a spoon. Bake for 25 minutes, until golden, well risen and a skewer inserted into the centre of the cakes comes out clean. Leave to rest in the tins for 3–4 minutes, then carefully turn out onto a wire rack and leave until cold.

MAKE AND ICE THE BISCUITS

4. Make the shortbread dough following the instructions on page 20. Line a baking sheet with baking parchment.

5. Roll out the dough on a lightly floured work surface to 2–3mm thick and use the template on page 14 to cut out a spade shape. Arrange on the prepared baking sheet.

6. Use the base of the 18cm cake tin as a guide to cut out a 2cm-wide rainbow-shaped strip from the dough and carefully transfer it to the baking sheet. This will be the handle for your bucket.

7. Using the cutters, stamp out seaside shapes from the remaining dough and lay them on the baking sheet. Chill all the biscuits for 30 minutes. Preheat the oven to 180°C/160°C fan/gas mark 4.

8. Bake the biscuits for 12–15 minutes, or until golden brown. Leave to cool on the baking sheet for 10 minutes and then transfer to a wire rack and leave until cold.

9. Prepare the royal icing using the instructions on page 21, up to the end of step 3, so that it's thick enough to hold a firm ribbon trail when you lift the spoon. Spoon 3–4 tablespoons into a disposable piping bag and cover the remainder in cling film. Using the detailed instructions on page 21 to help you, snip the end of the piping bag to a fine point and pipe a thin, continuous outline around each biscuit. Leave to set for 20 minutes.

10. Divide the remaining royal icing between small bowls, adding a drop of water to each one. Use cocktail sticks dipped in food-colouring pastes to tint each one a different colour. Flood the middle section of each biscuit with different coloured icing and leave to set firm for at least 1 hour. Pipe details onto the biscuits using the white icing, add sugar pearls, if using, and leave to set.

ASSEMBLE THE CAKE

11. Prepare the vanilla buttercream following the instructions on page 22.

12. Use a large serrated knife to level the tops of the sponges. Spread the top of one of the large sponges with jam. Spread the underside of the second large sponge with buttercream and sandwich the two together. Repeat this layering with the smaller cakes. You will now have 4 layers of cake and 3 of jam and buttercream, with the large cakes on the bottom and the smaller cakes on top.

13. Using the same knife, trim the cakes at an angle, starting at the top and working down the sides, to make an upturned bucket shape. Save the scraps. Cover the whole cake with an even, smooth crumb coat layer of buttercream, filling in any gaps as you go. Reserve some buttercream for the top of the bucket.

DECORATE THE CAKE

14. Tint 700g of the fondant icing red and roll it out on a lightly dusted work surface to a disc about 2–3mm thick. Roll the icing around the rolling pin and carefully drape it over the cake to cover it evenly. Use your hands to smooth it over the sponge and trim off any excess from the base.

15. Tint the remaining fondant icing blue. Roll it out to 2mm thick and cut it into 3cm-wide strips. Lightly brush the strips with water and press them around the sides of the bucket at the top. Leave the icing to dry for about 1 hour, then turn the cake the right way up and spread the remaining buttercream over the top.

16. Scatter the crushed digestives onto a serving platter and arrange the bucket on top, right side up. Secure the handle biscuit on top of the bucket and cover the buttercream with digestive crumbs. Arrange the iced biscuits around and serve.

HOLLY'S CAMPING CAKE

SERVES 20–25

Making dens is such a universally favourite pastime for children; it's little surprise that most are enthusiastic about the prospect of pitching a real tent and sleeping under the stars. This camping-themed cake is perfect for a celebration, whatever the age of the recipient.

FOR THE VANILLA SPONGE

250g unsalted butter

250g caster sugar

2 teaspoons vanilla extract

4 eggs, lightly beaten

200g plain flour

50g cornflour

3 teaspoons baking powder

a pinch of salt

4 tablespoons milk

FOR THE BUTTERCREAM

250g unsalted butter

500g icing sugar

2 tablespoons milk

FOR THE DECORATION

500g white fondant icing

1kg brown fondant icing

green, yellow, grey and red food-colouring pastes

1 x tube white writing icing

50g double-chocolate sandwich cookies

cornflour, for dusting

cocoa powder, for dusting

YOU WILL ALSO NEED

cardboard, a ruler and sticky tape

cocktail stick

2 x 20cm round baking tins

string, for measuring

MAKE THE TENT AND BUNTING

1. The day before you plan to serve the cake, make the fondant tent. Using the diagram on page 14 as a guide, make a triangular cardboard tent (a cereal box is ideal for this). Cut a piece of card to 11 x 19cm and fold it in half for the roof. Cut a second piece to 10 x 11cm and fix it to the bottom edge of the roof using tape on the inside of the structure. Tape triangles of card to cover each end.

2. Break off 250g of the white fondant icing and tint it green using food-colouring paste. Use a cocktail stick to add drops of colour at a time and knead the colour into the fondant before adding more. Roll it out on a cornflour-dusted work surface to 3mm thick. Cut a rectangle 15 x 23cm and fix it onto the cardboard roof using a little water, allowing a 2mm overhang at each edge. Use a cocktail stick to create a 'stitching' pattern along the edges.

3. Cut 2 triangles of fondant to cover the ends of the tent and fix one in place using a little water. Cut the second triangle in half vertically to resemble the opening of a tent, create stitching along the edges and attach it to the tent. You can fix a little brown fondant under the tent flap if you wish to hide the cardboard, or even make little fondant feet to position poking out of the tent.

4. Make a tent window by cutting a piece of thinly rolled fondant to 5 x 5cm. Roll it up three-quarters of the way and fix the unrolled end to one side of the tent. Cut a thin belt to 'hold' the rolled window in place and create stitching along the top of the window.

5. To make the bunting, break off 100g fondant and tint it yellow. Roll it out to 3mm thick and cut out triangles. Use a toothpick to carve the name of the birthday girl or boy into the triangles. Fix these to the other side of the tent and cut a very thin piece of fondant 'string' to join them together. If you wish you can make little fondant bows for each end. Leave all the decorations overnight to set hard, wrapping any scraps of fondant in cling film to use later.

MAKE THE OTHER FONDANT DECORATIONS

6. Mould some of the remaining green fondant into wellington boot shapes. Insert a toothpick into the leg and move it in circles to create holes for feet.

7. To make a bonfire, roll sticks from brown fondant and carve lines into them to make them look like sticks. Tint 50g fondant grey and roll it into little stones. Tint 20g fondant red and roll red, yellow and orange (made by combining a little red and yellow) fondant to about 3mm thick and cut 4 'flames' from each – you won't need them all but they are prone to snapping. Leave to dry on a rack for 1 hour.

8. Make a sign using brown fondant rolled to about 1cm thick. Cut the edges into zig-zags and create a wood effect using a sharp knife. Leave to dry for 1 hour and then pipe the age of the birthday boy or girl onto it using the tube of white writing icing. Roll a post about 3 x 2cm from another piece of brown fondant.

9. Make little acorns using brown and a light brown fondant (mix a little yellow into brown fondant to lighten it). Roll a sphere for the acorn from the lighter colour. Take a small piece of the darker brown fondant and squash it into a circle. Fix this to the top of the acorn. Lightly cross-hatch the top and fix a small stalk. Leave to dry.

10. Make mushrooms by moulding white fondant into 2 x 2cm cylinder shapes that taper to be a little wider at the bottom. Mould mushroom tops and fix them to the bases with a little water. Leave to dry.

MAKE THE VANILLA SPONGE

11. Preheat the oven to 180°C/160°C fan/gas mark 4 and position the shelves as close to the middle as possible, leaving enough space between them for the cakes to rise. Grease the cake tins and line the bases with discs of buttered baking parchment.

12. Make the vanilla sponge mix following the instructions on page 17, up to the end of step 3.

13. Divide the batter evenly between the prepared tins and spread the mixture level with a palette knife or the back of a spoon. Bake for 30–35 minutes until golden, well risen and a skewer inserted into the centre of the sponges comes out clean. Leave to rest in the tins for 3–4 minutes and then carefully turn out the cakes onto a wire rack and leave until cold.

ASSEMBLE THE CAKE

14. Make the buttercream following the instructions on page 22.

15. Use a little buttercream to fix the base sponge layer to a cake board or stand. Spread a thin layer of buttercream over the sponge and fix the second layer on top. Spread with more buttercream and top with the final layer. Cover the entire cake with a thin layer of buttercream.

16. Roll a piece of brown fondant into a circle approximately 1½cm thick and 1cm wider all round than the cake. Use a knife to carve half circles into the fondant and then cut lines from the centre outwards so that it resembles the top of a tree stump. Lay this over the top of the cake and press the overhang over the edges of the sponge to sit flush to the side of the cake.

17. Measure the depth and circumference of the cake using a piece of string. Roll out a piece of brown fondant to the length of the circumference and about 5mm taller than the height of the cake. It should be 1cm thick. Gently press around the cake, sealing the seams with a little water. Carve 'knots' and wood grain and rub a little cocoa powder into the deeper cuts in the top of the 'log' to look like dirt.

18. Arrange the fondant tent, boots, bonfire and sign on top of the cake, using a little water to fix the sign to the post and the decorations to the stump. You do not need to attach the tent as this won't be eaten. Grind the chocolate cookies to fine crumbs and scatter around the base. Place the acorns and mushrooms in the cookie soil. Dust a little cocoa over the tops of the mushrooms and serve.

FONDANT ICING DRIES OUT WHEN EXPOSED TO THE AIR, SO WRAP ANY YOU'RE NOT WORKING WITH IN CLING FILM UNTIL REQUIRED.

BUNTING CAKE

SERVES 16–20

This is a simple and traditional vanilla sponge filled with buttercream and jam and iced in fondant icing. The bunting can be decorated to match your party colours and even spell out the name of the birthday boy or girl.

FOR THE VANILLA SPONGE (2 BATCHES)

2 x 350g unsalted butter

2 x 350g caster sugar

2 x 2 teaspoons vanilla extract

2 x 6 eggs, lightly beaten

2 x 300g plain flour

2 x 50g cornflour

2 x 4 teaspoons baking powder

2 x pinch of salt

2 x 4 tablespoons milk

400g seedless raspberry or apricot jam or lemon curd

FOR THE VANILLA BUTTERCREAM

250g unsalted butter

500g icing sugar, sifted

2 teaspoons vanilla extract

2–3 tablespoons milk

FOR THE DECORATION

1kg ready-roll white fondant icing

string, for measuring

200g sugarpaste or fondant icing

assorted food-colouring pastes

100g royal icing sugar, plus extra for dusting

YOU WILL ALSO NEED

2 x 23cm round cake tins

2 x 15cm round cake tins

disposable piping bag

ribbons and fancy string

MAKE THE VANILLA SPONGES

1. Preheat the oven to 180°C/160°C fan/gas mark 4 and position the shelves as close to the middle as possible, leaving enough space between them for the cakes to rise. Grease the 23cm cake tins and line the bases with discs of buttered baking parchment.

2. You will need to make up 2 batches of the vanilla sponge mix using the ingredients listed left and following the instructions on page 17. Make up the first batch and divide evenly between the prepared 23cm tins, spreading the mixture level with a palette knife or the back of a spoon. Bake for 30–35 minutes until golden, well risen and a skewer inserted into the centre of the sponges comes out clean. Leave to rest in the tins for 3–4 minutes and then carefully turn out onto a wire rack and leave until cold. Wash and dry one of the tins and grease and line it along with the 15cm tins.

3. Make up the second batch of cake mix and divide between the prepared tins. Bake the larger cake for 30 minutes and the smaller ones for 20–25 minutes. Leave to cool on a wire rack before either icing or covering with cling film until ready to finish.

ASSEMBLE THE CAKE

4. Prepare the vanilla buttercream using the instructions on page 22. Cover and set aside at room temperature until needed.

5. Lay the sponges on a work surface and use a large serrated knife to level the tops. Spread the top of one of the large sponges with jam or lemon curd and the underside of a second layer with buttercream. Sandwich the two together. Repeat to make a stack of 3 large sponge layers sandwiched with jam and buttercream.

6. Spread one of the smaller sponge layers with buttercream and jam and top it with the second small sponge.

7. Use a palette knife to spread a thin crumb coat layer of buttercream over the top and sides of both cake stacks, spreading it smoothly and using the buttercream to fill any gaps or holes.

DECORATE THE CAKE

8. Use a length of string to measure the distance from the base of the large cake stack over the top and down to the bottom edge on the other side. Use this as a guide to roll out two-thirds of the white fondant on a lightly dusted work surface to a neat disc the same width. Carefully roll the fondant over the rolling pin and drape it over the cake stack to cover it evenly, unrolling it from the rolling pin as you do so. Smooth the icing into place with your hands and use a sharp knife to trim off any excess from the bottom.

9. Use the remaining fondant to cover the small cake stack in the same way. Leave both cakes for at least 1 hour for the icing to dry and harden.

MAKE THE BUNTING

10. Divide the sugarpaste or ready-roll fondant into 3 or 4 even portions. Use food-colouring pastes, added in tiny amounts with a cocktail stick, to tint each portion of icing a different colour, kneading the colour in well before adding more. Cover each portion in cling film. Lightly scrunch up some baking parchment and lay it on the work surface.

11. Take 1 portion of sugarpaste or fondant and roll it out on a work surface lightly dusted with icing sugar to about 2mm thick. Use a sharp knife to cut out 2–3cm-long triangles and arrange them on the scrunched baking parchment, gently pressing each triangle into the folds to shape it. Repeat with the other colours and leave to dry for at least 1 hour. Sugarpaste will dry quicker and firmer than fondant icing.

DECORATE THE CAKE

12. Mix the royal icing following the instructions on page 21 to make a smooth icing that just holds a ribbon trail. Scoop into a disposable piping bag and snip the end to a fine point.

13. Place the larger cake on a cake stand and top with the smaller cake, making sure it is centred. Wrap a length of ribbon around the bottom edge of the cake and another around the middle where the 2 cakes meet. Secure the ribbon at the back of the cakes with a dot of royal icing.

14. Using a dot of royal icing on the underside of each triangle, stick the flags all around the sides of each cake, spacing each one slightly apart so that it looks like billowing bunting. Lay a length of fine ribbon or fancy string across the top of the bunting, using dots of royal icing to keep it in place. Decorate the top of the cake with a bunting topper and serve.

RIBBON WRAPPED AROUND THE BASE OF CAKES IS A CUNNING WAY OF HIDING ANY UNTIDY JOINS.

FLOWER GARDEN

SERVES 12

Mary Mary quite contrary... how many biscuits does your garden grow? Let your imagination run wild when decorating this cake and use a variety of flower cutters.

FOR THE VANILLA SPONGE

250g unsalted butter

250g caster sugar

2 teaspoons vanilla extract

4 eggs, lightly beaten

200g plain flour

50g cornflour

3 teaspoons baking powder

a pinch of salt

4 tablespoons milk

6 tablespoons jam

FOR THE SHORTBREAD BISCUITS

225g unsalted butter

150g icing sugar

1 egg, lightly beaten

grated zest of ½ unwaxed lemon

1 teaspoon vanilla bean paste

350g plain flour, plus extra for dusting

½ teaspoon baking powder

a pinch of salt

FOR THE VANILLA BUTTERCREAM

250g unsalted butter

500g icing sugar

2 tablespoons milk

green food-colouring paste

FOR THE DECORATION

500g royal icing sugar

assorted food-colouring pastes

mimosa sugar balls

YOU WILL ALSO NEED

3 x 20cm round cake tins

2 x baking sheets

assorted flower, snail and caterpillar cutters

baking sheet

paper food-grade lolly sticks or wooden skewers

disposable piping bags

MAKE THE VANILLA SPONGE

1. Preheat the oven to 180°C/160°C fan/gas mark 4 and position the shelves as close to the middle as possible, leaving enough space between them for the cakes to rise. Grease the cake tins and line the bases with discs of buttered baking parchment.

2. Make the vanilla sponge mix following the instructions on page 17, up to the end of step 3.

3. Divide the cake mix evenly between the prepared tins and spread it level with a palette knife or the back of a spoon. Bake for 20 minutes until golden, well risen and a skewer inserted into the centre of the sponges comes out clean. Leave to rest in the tins for 3–4 minutes and then carefully turn out onto a wire rack and leave until cold.

MAKE AND DECORATE THE BISCUITS

4. Make the shortbread mix following the instructions on page 20. Line a baking sheet with baking parchment.

5. Divide the chilled dough into 2 and roll out half to 2mm thick on a lightly dusted work surface. Use a large knife to cut out several 1 x 9cm fence posts – they can be a little uneven for a vintage fence look. You will need about 31–32 posts. Arrange on the prepared baking sheet and chill for 15 minutes.

6. Roll out the remaining dough to 2mm thick and stamp out a caterpillar and snail, if you have cutters, and as many flower shapes as you can in assorted shapes and sizes. Lay on the baking sheets and press a lolly stick or skewer into each flower. Chill for a further 15 minutes before baking all the biscuits for about 12 minutes, until pale golden. Leave to cool on wire racks until completely cold.

7. Prepare the royal icing following the instructions on page 21. Set aside half and divide the remainder into 4 or 5 bowls. Tint each bowl a different colour. Ice the picket fence posts with white icing and then ice and decorate the flowers following the instructions on page 21. Use drops of icing to attach mimosa sugar balls to the centres of some of the flowers.

ASSEMBLE THE CAKE

8. Make the vanilla buttercream following the instructions on page 22. Tint half of it green and set it aside.

9. Lay the sponge layers on the work surface and use a large serrated knife to level the tops. Place one layer on a serving plate and spread it with jam and white buttercream. Repeat with the remaining layers and then cover the whole cake with the green buttercream.

10. Press the picket fence posts all around the edge of the cake. Push the flower cookies into the top, positioning them at different heights, and add the snail and caterpillar around the edge before serving.

SAILBOAT CAKE

SERVES 12–16

*A flotilla of shortbread yachts race across a choppy sea of buttercream!
You could decorate these yachts with the name and age of the birthday boy or
girl if you like. Watch out for the seagulls – they'll swoop on the sandwiches
when you're not looking.*

FOR THE VANILLA SPONGE

350g unsalted butter

350g caster sugar

2 teaspoons vanilla extract

6 eggs, lightly beaten

300g plain flour

50g cornflour

4 teaspoons baking powder

a pinch of salt

5 tablespoons milk

3 tablespoons raspberry or apricot jam

FOR THE SHORTBREAD BISCUITS

225g unsalted butter

150g icing sugar

1 egg, lightly beaten

grated zest of ½ unwaxed lemon

1 teaspoon vanilla bean paste

350g plain flour, plus extra for dusting

½ teaspoon baking powder

a pinch of salt

FOR THE MERINGUE BUTTERCREAM

250g caster sugar

4 egg whites

2 tablespoons water

1 teaspoon vanilla extract

a pinch of salt

325g unsalted butter

FOR THE DECORATION

500g royal icing sugar

blue and red food-colouring pastes

blue and white sprinkles

YOU WILL ALSO NEED

2 x 23cm round springform cake tins

sailboat or yacht biscuit cutter

baking sheets

3 x disposable piping bags

MAKE THE VANILLA SPONGE

1. Preheat the oven to 180°C/160°C fan/gas mark 4
and position the shelves as close to the middle as possible,
leaving enough space between them for the cakes to rise.
Grease the cake tins and line the bases with discs
of buttered baking parchment.

2. Make the vanilla sponge mix following the instructions
on page 17, up to the end of step 3.

3. Divide the cake mix evenly between the prepared tins
and spread level with a palette knife or the back of a spoon.
Bake for 20 minutes until golden, well risen and a skewer
inserted into the centre of the sponges comes out clean.
Leave to rest in the tins for 3–4 minutes and then carefully
turn out onto a wire rack and leave until cold.

MAKE THE SHORTBREAD BOATS

4. Make the shortbread dough following the instructions on page 20. Line the baking sheets with baking parchment.

5. Roll out the chilled dough on a lightly floured work surface to about 2mm thick. Stamp out boat-shaped biscuits, re-rolling the scraps to make more, and arrange on the prepared baking sheets. Chill for 20 minutes.

6. Bake for about 12–15 minutes, until firm and pale golden. Leave to cool on the baking sheets.

DECORATE THE BOATS

7. Prepare the royal icing following the instructions on page 21, adding enough water to make a thick writing icing. Spoon 3 tablespoons into a small bowl and tint it red using food-colouring paste. Spoon another 2 tablespoons into a separate bowl and tint it blue. Cover both bowls and set aside.

8. Scoop 2 tablespoons of the white icing into a disposable piping bag, snip the end to a fine point and, using the instructions on page 21 to help you, pipe an outline of the sails onto each biscuit. Spoon the red icing into a second bag and pipe a red outline around the hull of the boats and a flag at the top of the mast. Leave to set for 15 minutes.

9. Scoop the red and white icings back into their bowls and add a drop of water to each. Use a teaspoon to flood the sails and hull between the outlines. Leave to set for 30 minutes.

10. Fill a third piping bag with blue icing and pipe numbers and details onto each yacht. Leave to set for a further 15 minutes.

ASSEMBLE THE CAKE

11. Make the meringue buttercream following the instructions on page 23.

12. Lay the sponges on the work surface and use a large serrated knife to level the tops. Place one of the layers on a serving plate and spread the top with a layer of jam. Spread the underside of the second sponge with 2–3 tablespoons of buttercream and sandwich the 2 cakes together.

13. Scoop half the buttercream into another bowl and set aside. Tint the remaining buttercream a pale shade of blue using the food-colouring paste and use a palette knife to cover the sides of the cake. Add a little blue colouring to the reserved buttercream and marble it through so that the colour is uneven. Use this to cover the top of the cake, spreading it into waves and swirls.

14. Scatter the top of the cake with sprinkles and position the sailboat biscuits on and around it to look as if they are racing across choppy seas.

HOT AIR BALLOON

SERVES 16–20

The skill here is in the decorative basketweave icing. This is simple enough to do, but does require a little practise to get right first time. Once mastered, it is very effective. See page 15 for a handy diagram.

FOR THE CHOCOLATE SPONGE

300g unsalted butter, plus extra for greasing

300g caster sugar

100g soft light brown sugar

2 teaspoons vanilla extract

6 eggs, lightly beaten

375g plain flour

80g cocoa powder

4 teaspoons baking powder

a pinch of salt

100ml whole milk

120ml boiling water

FOR THE CHOCOLATE BUTTERCREAM

500g unsalted butter

1kg icing sugar, sifted

150g cocoa powder, sifted

5 tablespoons milk

2 tablespoons golden syrup

3 teaspoons vanilla extract

YOU WILL ALSO NEED

2 x 20cm square cake tins

disposable piping bag

basket weave nozzle

cake toppers or skewers

small helium-filled balloons

ribbon

MAKE THE CHOCOLATE SPONGE

1. Preheat the oven to 180°C/160°C fan/gas mark 4 and position the shelves as close to the middle as possible, leaving enough space between them for the cakes to rise. Grease the cake tins and line the bases with squares of buttered baking parchment.

2. Make the chocolate sponge mix following the instructions on page 18, up to the end of step 3.

3. Divide the cake mix evenly between the prepared tins and level with a palette knife or the back of a spoon. Bake for 30 minutes, until well risen and a skewer inserted into the centre of the cakes comes out clean. Leave to rest in the tins for 3–4 minutes and then carefully turn out onto a wire rack and leave until cold.

ASSEMBLE AND DECORATE THE CAKE

4. Make the chocolate buttercream following the instructions on page23.

5. Lay the sponges on the work surface and use a large serrated knife to level the tops, then cut each sponge in half horizontally to make 4 layers. Spread one of the layers with buttercream and top with a second layer. Repeat to make one large cake. Cover the whole cake with a thin crumb coat of buttercream and chill for 30 minutes.

YOU'LL NEED TO CONCENTRATE ONCE YOU START TO PIPE THE BASKETWEAVE BUTTERCREAM SO TURN OFF THE PHONE AND AVOID ALL DISTRACTIONS AS IT'S VERY EASY TO LOSE YOUR PLACE AND RHYTHM.

TRY PERFECTING THE BASKETWEAVE TECHNIQUE ON A PIECE OF BAKING PARCHMENT BEFORE YOU TACKLE THE CAKE.

6. Fit the piping bag with the nozzle and fill it with buttercream. Using the diagram on page 15 as a guide, first pipe a single vertical stripe of icing all the way down one side of the cake. Now pipe short horizontal strips across this vertical, each one a nozzle-width apart and then pipe a second vertical stripe up against the first one to cover the ends. Pipe horizontal strips across this second vertical, starting up against the edge of the first stripe and fitting each one in between the first set of horizontals. Repeat until the sides of the cake are covered in buttercream and then pipe along the edges of the cake to neaten it.

7. Stick skewers or cake toppers into each corner of the cake to make flagpoles and tie helium-filled balloons to each pole, decorating each one with a ribbon bow. Tie the balloons into a bunch and serve.

CIRCUS TENT

This cake does take a little time and space to decorate, but the effort is more than worth it. As a centrepiece to a circus-themed party this should have the clowns turning somersaults!

FOR THE CHOCOLATE SPONGE (2 BATCHES)

2 × 200g unsalted butter, plus extra for greasing
2 × 150g caster sugar
2 × 65g soft light brown sugar
2 × 2 teaspoons vanilla extract
2 × 4 eggs, lightly beaten
2 × 250g plain flour
2 × 50g cocoa
2 × 3 teaspoons baking powder
a pinch of salt
2 × 75ml whole milk
2 × 75ml boiling water

FOR THE VANILLA BUTTERCREAM

250g unsalted butter
500g icing sugar
1 teaspoon vanilla bean paste
2–3 tablespoons milk

FOR THE DECORATION

1kg ready-roll fondant icing
red, blue, yellow and black food-colouring pastes
icing sugar, for dusting

YOU WILL ALSO NEED

2 × 18cm round cake tins
large disposable piping bag
long skewer
string, for measuring
crimp-edged pasta wheel
small 3–4cm cutter
paper flag
circus figures

MAKE THE CHOCOLATE SPONGE

1. Preheat the oven to 180°C/160°C fan/gas mark 4 and position the shelves as close to the middle as possible, leaving enough space between them for the cakes to rise. Grease the tins with butter and line the bases with discs of buttered baking parchment.

2. Make the first batch of chocolate sponge mix following the instructions on page 18, up to the end of step 3.

3. Divide equally between the prepared tins and spread level with a palette knife or the back of a spoon. Bake for 30 minutes until well risen and a skewer inserted into the centre of the sponges comes out clean. Leave to rest in the tins for 3–4 minutes and then carefully turn out onto a wire rack and leave until cold. Wash, grease and re-line the tins and make the second batch of sponges. Once completely cold, wrap all the sponges in cling film and set aside.

ASSEMBLE THE CAKE

4. Make the vanilla buttercream following the instructions on page 17. Fill the piping bag and snip the end to make a 1cm hole.

5. Unwrap the sponge layers and lay them on the work surface. Use a large serrated knife to trim the tops of 3 of the sponges to level them. Spread these layers with jam and pipe 3–4 tablespoons of buttercream over each one, spreading them level with a palette knife. Stack the 3 layers.

6. Insert a skewer into the exact centre of the fourth sponge – this will be your centre marker. Using a serrated knife, trim the sponge all round from the centre marker to the bottom edge to make a smooth dome. Remove the skewer.

7. Place the sponge dome on top of the stacked layers and use a palette knife to spread the remaining buttercream over the top and sides of the cake in an even crumb coat layer.

DECORATE THE TENT

8. Break off 50g of the fondant icing and colour it black using the food-colouring paste. Use a piece of string to measure the height of the bottom 3 layers of sponge and roll out the fondant on a lightly dusted work surface to a neat rectangle the same height and 12cm wide. Position on the side of the cake – this will be the tent opening.

9. Use the string to measure the circumference of the cake. Roll out 400g of the white fondant to a neat rectangle slightly longer and wider than the height and circumference of the bottom 3 sponge layers. Trim the edges to neaten them and roll up the icing from the shorter end, trying not to stretch it. Hold the long edge at the middle of the black icing rectangle and carefully unroll the icing around the cake, gently pressing it to stick it to the buttercream and the top of the black icing.

10. Take 250g of the fondant and tint it red. Break off one-third, cover and set aside. Roll out the remaining two-thirds to a neat rectangle the same height as the white icing and about 1–2mm thick (it doesn't need to be as long). Trim the long edges to neaten them and then cut into 1–2cm strips using the pasta wheel. Lightly brush the white fondant with water and, starting at one end, carefully position the red strips around the cake to make stripes. Gently curve out the ends of the white icing to resemble the entrance to a circus tent.

11. Tint 125g of the fondant blue and roll it out to a long strip the same length as the circumference of the cake and about 2cm wide. Use a small round cutter to create a scalloped edge along the bottom edge. Carefully roll up the fondant. Very lightly brush the top edge of the striped fondant with a little water and attach the blue scalloped band to it.

12. Use the string to measure the width of the dome top, from the top of the fondant icing to the opposite edge. Roll out 175g of white fondant to a neat circle slightly wider than this measurement. Cut out a neat disc. Carefully fold the disc in half and then in half again and position it on top of the cake, unfolding and gently smoothing it with your hands. There will be a little bit hanging over the edges.

13. Roll out the remaining red icing to the same size (it will be a little thinner). Use a knife to cut the red disc into neat even wedges. Lightly brush the top of the cake with water and position the red triangles evenly around it.

14. Use scissors to trim the edges of the circus roof to neaten them and crimp them between your fingers as if you were making a pie crust. Top with a paper flag and serve surrounded by circus figures.

SIMPLE CAKES

Sometimes you want a party cake without all the bells and whistles, either to accompany a highly decorated cake for a large crowd or as the showstopper itself. The following simple but very delicious cakes require almost no decorative skill, but pack a punch in the flavour department that will delight party guests of all ages.

CARROT CAKE

SERVES 10–12

Packed full of flavour, but still light in texture, this quick-mix cake is so easy to make. Top it with banana or toasted coconut chips for an easy decoration, or make marzipan carrots if you prefer.

FOR THE CAKE

200g grated carrot

finely grated zest of 1 orange

2 small or 1 large ripe banana, mashed

30g desiccated coconut

3 eggs

250ml sunflower oil

250g golden caster sugar

1–2 tablespoons milk

1 teaspoon vanilla bean paste or extract

325g plain flour

2 teaspoons baking powder

½ teaspoon bicarbonate of soda

½ teaspoon ground cinnamon

a pinch of salt

FOR THE CREAM CHEESE FROSTING

350g full-fat cream cheese

juice of ½ orange

2–3 rounded tablespoons runny honey

50g coconut chips, lightly toasted

YOU WILL ALSO NEED

2 x 20cm round cake tins

MAKE THE CAKE

1. Preheat the oven to 180°C/160°C fan/gas mark 4 and position the shelf as close to the middle as possible. Grease the cake tins and line the bases with discs of buttered baking parchment.

2. Tip the grated carrot, orange zest, mashed banana and desiccated coconut into a bowl and mix to combine.

3. In a separate bowl, whisk the eggs, sunflower oil, sugar, milk and vanilla bean paste or extract until smooth. Add the carrot mixture and mix well.

4. Sift the flour, baking powder, bicarbonate of soda, ground cinnamon and salt into the bowl and mix well using a large spoon or rubber spatula until thoroughly combined.

5. Divide the mixture evenly between the prepared tins and spread them level with a spatula or the back of a spoon. Bake for about 30 minutes, or until a skewer inserted into the centre of the cakes comes out clean. Cool in the tins for 10 minutes before turning out onto a wire rack. Turn the cakes the right way up and leave to cool completely.

ASSEMBLE THE LAYERS

6. To make the frosting, beat the cream cheese, orange juice and honey together until smooth.

7. Level the top of one of the sponge layers, if necessary, with a large serrated knife and lay it on a serving plate. Top with half the cream cheese frosting, spreading it almost to the edges with a palette knife. Top with the second layer and spread with the remaining frosting. Scatter with toasted coconut chips to serve.

GLUTEN & DAIRY FREE LEMON, ALMOND & RASPBERRY CAKE

SERVES 10–12

This cake is not only delicious, but couldn't be easier to make as it is all mixed together at once – dairy free spread is so soft and light that it makes creaming unnecessary. If you want to omit the nuts, simply replace the ground almonds with the same quantity of flour and use soya or rice milk in place of almond milk.

225g caster sugar

200g dairy free (sunflower or soya) spread

3 eggs

250g gluten-free self-raising flour

50g ground almonds

50g desiccated coconut

zest and juice of 2 unwaxed lemons

zest and juice of 1 unwaxed lime

100ml almond or soya milk

100g granulated sugar

300g fresh raspberries

icing sugar, for dusting

YOU WILL ALSO NEED

1 x 20cm round springform cake tin

1. Preheat the oven to 180°C/160°C fan/gas mark 4 and position the shelf as close to the middle as possible. Grease the cake tin with dairy free spread and line the base with a disc of greased baking parchment.

2. Tip the sugar, dairy free spread, eggs, flour, ground almonds and desiccated coconut into a large bowl or the bowl of a stand mixer and mix with a wooden spoon, or on a medium-high speed for about 2 minutes, until thoroughly combined. Add the lemon and lime zest along with the almond milk and mix again until smooth.

3. Scoop the cake mix into the prepared tin and spread it level with a palette knife or the back of a spoon. Bake for 35–40 minutes or until well risen, golden brown and a skewer inserted into the centre of the cake comes out clean. Sit the tin on a wire rack and leave to cool for 10 minutes.

4. In a small bowl, mix the lemon and lime juice with the granulated sugar. Prick all over the top of the cake with a skewer and slowly spoon over the citrus sugar, allowing the juice to seep into the holes and the sugar to rest on the top of the cake. Leave to cool completely before removing from the tin.

5. To serve, cover the top of the cake with fresh raspberries and lightly dust with icing sugar.

BANANA CAKE WITH CARAMEL PEANUT POPCORN

SERVES 12

You can use smooth or crunchy peanut butter for this recipe – whatever you prefer or happen to have in the cupboard. The same applies to the chocolate chips, which can be milk or dark. But whatever else happens, your bananas must be ripe – the riper the better in fact. Under-ripe bananas will not only be hard to mash to a smooth pulp, but will also be lacking in the flavour department. At a push you could use ready made caramel popcorn to adorn this cake, but homemade is really easy and far more delicious.

FOR THE CAKE

175g unsalted butter

50g peanut butter

200g golden caster sugar

1 teaspoon vanilla extract or vanilla bean paste

4 eggs, lightly beaten

4 medium very ripe bananas

3 tablespoons soured cream

225g plain flour

50g cornflour

2 teaspoons baking powder

1 teaspoon bicarbonate of soda

a pinch of salt

100g chocolate chips

FOR THE POPCORN

1 tablespoon sunflower oil

50g popcorn kernels

100g caster sugar

40g unsalted butter

1 teaspoon vanilla extract

75g salted peanuts, roughly chopped

FOR THE FUDGE FROSTING

75g dark chocolate, chopped

75g milk chocolate, chopped

25g unsalted butter

4 tablespoons whipping cream

2 tablespoons golden syrup

YOU WILL ALSO NEED

2.5-litre Bundt or kugelhopf tin

large baking tray

MAKE THE CAKE

1. Preheat the oven to 180°C/160°C fan/gas mark 4 and position the shelf just below the middle. Pop the cake tin in the freezer for 5 minutes, or the fridge for 15 minutes. Melt 25g of the butter and brush it liberally all over the inside of the cold cake tin, making sure you grease all the creases, nooks and crannies.

2. In a large bowl or the bowl of a stand mixer, beat the rest of the butter, the peanut butter, caster sugar and vanilla extract or paste until pale and light. Scrape down the sides of the bowl and gradually add the beaten eggs, mixing well between each addition and scraping down the sides of the bowl from time to time.

3. In a small bowl, mash the bananas with a fork until almost smooth, add the soured cream and mix to combine.

4. Sift the flour, cornflour, baking powder, bicarbonate of soda and salt into the mixing bowl. Add the mashed banana mixture and beat again until smooth and thoroughly combined. Add the chocolate chips and fold them into the batter.

5. Spoon the cake mix into the prepared tin and spread it level with the back of a spoon. Bake for 45–50 minutes until golden brown, well risen and a skewer inserted into the widest part of the cake comes out clean. Leave to cool in the tin for 20 minutes and then turn out onto a wire rack and leave until cold.

MAKE THE CARAMEL POPCORN

6. Meanwhile, heat the sunflower oil in a large saucepan over a high heat. Add the popcorn kernels and cover with a lid. Shake the pan from time to time as soon as the popping starts and cook until it stops. Tip the popcorn into a large bowl and pick out any un-popped kernels. Line the baking tray with parchment paper.

7. Tip the sugar into a small, heavy bottomed pan with 2 tablespoons water. Set the pan over a low–medium heat and leave, without stirring or boiling the water, until all the sugar dissolves, then increase the heat and bring the syrup to a boil, continuing to cook, without stirring, until the sugar starts to turn into an amber caramel. Swirl the pan to ensure that it cooks evenly.

8. Remove the pan from the heat, add the butter and vanilla extract and stir to combine. Quickly pour the buttery caramel over the popcorn, add the chopped peanuts and mix to combine. Tip onto the prepared baking tray and set aside until cold.

DECORATE THE CAKE

9. Tip all the chocolate into a heatproof bowl and melt over a pan of barely simmering water, making sure the bottom doesn't touch the water, or in the microwave on a low setting. Add the butter, cream and golden syrup and mix to combine. Leave to cool for 20–30 minutes.

10. Spoon the chocolate sauce over the banana cake, allowing it to drizzle over the sides, and leave to set for 20 minutes. Scatter the popcorn over the top of the cake and serve.

CHILLING THE CAKE TIN BEFORE YOU GREASE IT MAKES IT EASY TO SEE IF YOU'VE MISSED A SPOT.

BAKE OFF
BAKER'S
RECIPE

MIRANDA'S MILK CHOCOLATE BROWNIE CAKE

SERVES 16–20

Three layers of delicious chocolate brownie sandwiched with pale buttercream, rolled in sprinkles and topped with an indulgent milk chocolate ganache and a circle of much-loved nostalgic sweets. Covered with sparklers or candles this makes a perfect party cake!

FOR THE GANACHE

150g milk chocolate
150ml double cream

FOR THE BROWNIE MIX

340g good-quality milk chocolate, melted
400g unsalted butter
500g icing sugar
6 eggs
220g plain flour

FOR THE VANILLA BUTTERCREAM

450g icing sugar
225g unsalted butter
4 tablespoons semi-skimmed milk
1 teaspoon vanilla bean paste or vanilla extract

FOR THE DECORATION

rainbow sprinkles
malted milk chocolate-coated balls, chopped
sugar-coated chocolate drops, chopped

YOU WILL ALSO NEED

3 x 18cm round shallow loose-bottomed cake tins
large baking tray

MAKE THE GANACHE

1. Before making the cakes, put the chocolate and cream into a heatproof bowl set over a pan of barely simmering water, making sure the bottom of the bowl doesn't touch the water. Once the chocolate has melted, stir to combine, remove from the heat and leave at room temperature for a bit to firm up.

MAKE THE BROWNIE LAYERS

2. Preheat the oven to 180°C/160°C fan/gas mark 4 and position the shelves as close to the middle as possible, leaving enough space between them for the cakes to rise. Grease the cake tins and line the bases with discs of buttered baking parchment.

3. Melt the chocolate in a heatproof bowl set over a pan of barely simmering water, making sure the bottom doesn't touch the water, or in the microwave on a low setting, and set aside.

4. Cream the butter and icing sugar until light, creamy and fluffy. Add the eggs, one at a time, whisking well after each one. Gradually add the flour and beat until very smooth. Slowly pour in the melted chocolate and mix thoroughly.

5. Divide the mixture between the prepared tins and bake for about 30–35 minutes. Leave to cool in the tins until completely cold.

ASSEMBLE THE CAKE

6. Vigorously mix together all the ingredients for the buttercream to make it extra smooth and creamy.

7. Once all the brownie layers are cold, place the bottom layer on a circle of non-stick baking parchment and cover it with a layer of buttercream. Repeat with the second layer and place the third layer on top, then chill for 20–30 minutes to firm up a little.

8. Spread the sprinkles over the baking tray and roll the chilled cake in them, on its side, so that the sprinkles stick to the buttercream. Use a small blob of ganache to stick the cake to a cake stand or plate.

9. Spread the top of the cake with ganache, encouraging it to drip over the sides a little using the palette knife. Sprinkle broken sweeties around the top edge of the cake and serve.

LEMON SHERBET CAKE

If you prefer you can make this as a two-layer cake, but you will need to cook the sponges for a few minutes longer. For the filling, use the best lemon curd you can find, or use homemade, as they will have a more zingy lemon flavour.

FOR THE SPONGE

225g unsalted butter

225g caster sugar

4 eggs, lightly beaten

200g plain flour

25g cornflour

3 teaspoons baking powder

a pinch of salt

finely grated zest of 1 lemon

2 tablespoons milk

300g lemon curd

FOR THE LEMON BUTTERCREAM

200g unsalted butter

400g icing sugar, sifted

50g sherbet

finely grated zest of 1 lemon

FOR THE DECORATION

a handful of lemon sherbet sweets, roughly chopped

YOU WILL ALSO NEED

3 x 20cm round cake tins

MAKE THE SPONGE LAYERS

1. Preheat the oven to 180°C/160°C fan/gas mark 4 and position the shelves as close to the middle as possible, leaving enough space between them for the cakes to rise. Grease the cake tins and line the bases with discs of buttered baking parchment.

2. In a large bowl or the bowl of a stand mixer, cream the butter with the caster sugar until pale and light. Scrape down the sides of the bowl and mix again. Gradually add the beaten eggs, mixing well between each addition and scraping down the sides of the bowl from time to time.

3. Sift the flour, cornflour, baking powder and salt into the bowl and mix until just combined. Add the finely grated lemon zest and milk and beat again until silky smooth.

4. Divide the cake mix evenly between the prepared tins and spread them level with a palette knife or the back of a spoon. Bake for 15 minutes, until well risen, golden brown and a skewer inserted into the centre of the sponges comes out clean. Leave to cool in the tins for 3 minutes and then turn out onto a wire rack and leave until cold.

DECORATE THE CAKE

5. Make the lemon buttercream following the instructions for vanilla buttercream on page 17, adding the sherbet and lemon zest along with the icing sugar.

6. Place one of the sponge layers on a serving plate and spread it with a third of the buttercream and half the lemon curd. Lay another sponge on top, spread with more buttercream and curd and top with the final layer.

7. Spread the remaining buttercream over the top of the cake and scatter the chopped lemon sherbet sweets around the edge of the buttercream to serve.

IAN'S BANOFFEE CAKE

SERVES 12–16

This recipe is a twist on the classic banoffee pie. I was introduced to dulce de leche in Chile and fell in love with it. Rich, creamy and very sweet... what's not to love? If you can't find any, use tinned caramel instead. The key to the success of this recipe is to make sure the bananas are sweet and very ripe to really build up the sugar levels.

FOR THE SPONGE

250g unsalted butter

140g caster sugar

1 x 397g tin dulce de leche, or tinned caramel

4 eggs

2 teaspoons vanilla extract or vanilla bean paste

½ teaspoon salt

3 or 4 very ripe bananas

280g self-raising flour

1½ teaspoons baking powder

FOR THE FILLING AND TOPPING

250ml double cream

25g icing sugar

1 teaspoon cocoa powder

YOU WILL ALSO NEED

2 x 20cm round cake tins

disposable piping bag

MAKE THE SPONGE

1. Preheat the oven to 200°C/180°C fan/gas mark 6. Grease and line the cake tins with buttered baking parchment.

2. In a large mixing bowl, beat together the butter, caster sugar and 250g of the dulce de leche until light and fluffy. Add the eggs, one at a time, making sure each one is fully incorporated before adding the next. Beat in the vanilla extract or paste and the salt.

3. Peel 2 of the bananas and roughly mash about 120g of the flesh with a fork, then incorporate it evenly into the mixture. Finally, sift the self-raising flour and baking powder into the bowl and mix to incorporate.

4. Divide the cake mix between the prepared tins and bake for about 25 minutes, until nice and brown. Remove from the oven, run a knife around the inside edge of the tin and leave to cool for about 10 minutes before turning out onto a wire rack to cool completely.

ASSEMBLE AND DECORATE THE CAKE

5. Lay one of the sponges on a serving plate and level the top with a large serrated knife. Slice the remaining bananas into chunky slices and place them all over the top of the sponge. Whip the cream with the icing sugar until quite firm and spoon over the bananas in a thick layer. Drizzle half the remaining dulce de leche over the top and place the second sponge layer on top. Spread with more cream, sift cocoa powder over the top and serve.

CHOCOLATE FUDGE CAKE

SERVES 10–12

Adding condensed milk, not only to the cake mixture but also to the frosting, gives this cake an extra fudginess. Although it looks dark and rich, it's actually light, chocolaty and totally moreish.

FOR THE SPONGE

125g unsalted butter
150ml sunflower oil
175g caster sugar
50g soft light brown sugar
100g condensed milk
4 eggs
2 teaspoons vanilla extract
300g plain flour
100g cocoa powder
2 teaspoons baking powder
1 teaspoon bicarbonate of soda
a pinch of salt
100g soured cream
100ml boiling water

FOR THE FROSTING

100g dark chocolate, chopped
225g unsalted butter
150g icing sugar
25g cocoa powder, sifted
100g condensed milk
1 teaspoon vanilla extract

FOR THE DECORATION

a handful of salted pretzels
6 vanilla cream chocolate sandwich biscuits

YOU WILL ALSO NEED

2 x 20cm round cake tins

MAKE THE SPONGE

1. Preheat the oven to 180°C/160°C fan/gas mark 4 and position the shelves as close to the middle as possible, leaving enough space between them for the cakes to rise. Grease the cake tins and line the bases with discs of buttered baking parchment.

2. Melt the butter, let it cool slightly and pour it into a large bowl or the bowl of a stand mixer fitted with the whisk attachment. Add the sunflower oil, caster sugar, brown sugar, condensed milk, eggs and vanilla extract and beat well to combine.

3. Sift the flour, cocoa powder, baking powder, bicarbonate of soda and salt into the bowl. Add the soured cream and mix until smooth. Scrape down the sides of the bowl, slowly add the boiling water and mix again until thoroughly combined and silky smooth.

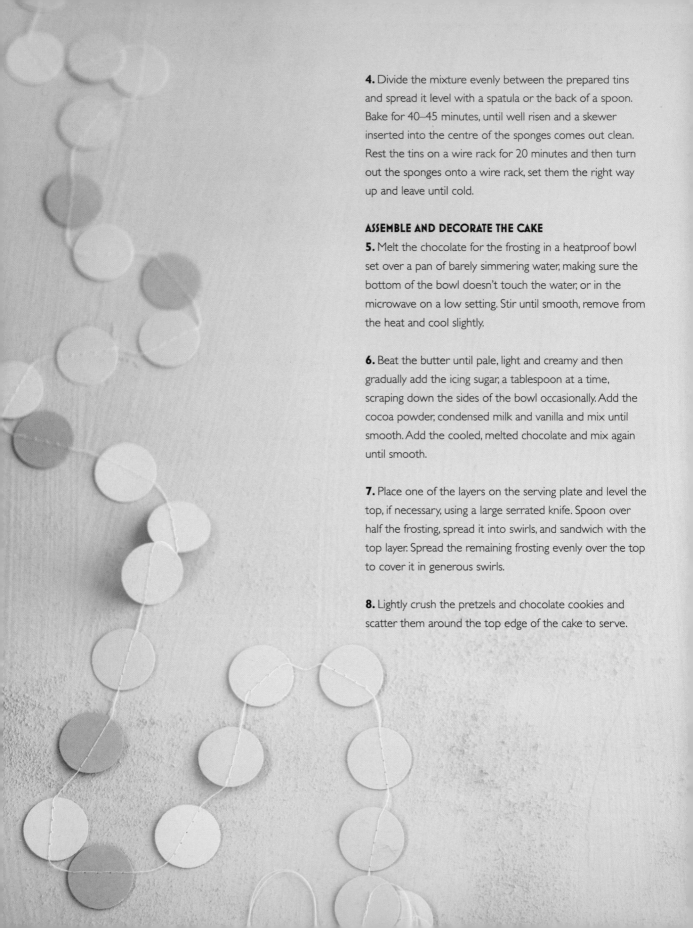

4. Divide the mixture evenly between the prepared tins and spread it level with a spatula or the back of a spoon. Bake for 40–45 minutes, until well risen and a skewer inserted into the centre of the sponges comes out clean. Rest the tins on a wire rack for 20 minutes and then turn out the sponges onto a wire rack, set them the right way up and leave until cold.

ASSEMBLE AND DECORATE THE CAKE

5. Melt the chocolate for the frosting in a heatproof bowl set over a pan of barely simmering water, making sure the bottom of the bowl doesn't touch the water, or in the microwave on a low setting. Stir until smooth, remove from the heat and cool slightly.

6. Beat the butter until pale, light and creamy and then gradually add the icing sugar, a tablespoon at a time, scraping down the sides of the bowl occasionally. Add the cocoa powder, condensed milk and vanilla and mix until smooth. Add the cooled, melted chocolate and mix again until smooth.

7. Place one of the layers on the serving plate and level the top, if necessary, using a large serrated knife. Spoon over half the frosting, spread it into swirls, and sandwich with the top layer. Spread the remaining frosting evenly over the top to cover it in generous swirls.

8. Lightly crush the pretzels and chocolate cookies and scatter them around the top edge of the cake to serve.

CHOCOLATE & VANILLA MARBLE CAKE

SERVES 10–12

This cake can be made a day in advance and iced and decorated on the day of the party. The ground almonds in the cake mix help to keep it moist.

FOR THE CHOCOLATE SPONGE

100g unsalted butter

100g caster sugar

40g soft light brown sugar

1 teaspoon vanilla extract

2 eggs, lightly beaten

100g plain flour

25g ground almonds

25g cocoa powder

1½ teaspoons baking powder

a pinch of salt

3 tablespoons boiling water

FOR THE VANILLA SPONGE

125g unsalted butter

125g caster sugar

2 teaspoons vanilla extract

2 eggs, lightly beaten

125g plain flour

25g cornflour

25g ground almonds

1½ teaspoons baking powder

a pinch of salt

3 tablespoons milk

FOR THE CHOCOLATE FUDGE FROSTING

75g dark chocolate

75g milk chocolate

25g unsalted butter

4 tablespoons whipping cream

2 tablespoons golden syrup

FOR THE DECORATION

350g malted chocolate balls and chocolate-coated caramels

chocolate pearl sprinkles

YOU WILL ALSO NEED

1 × 2lb loaf tin (23 × 8–9 × 8cm)

MAKE THE CHOCOLATE SPONGE MIX

1. Preheat the oven to 180°C/160°C fan/gas mark 4 and position the shelf as close to the middle as possible. Butter the inside of the loaf tin and line the base and ends with a strip of buttered baking parchment.

2. In a large bowl or the bowl of a stand mixer, cream the softened butter with the caster sugar, light brown sugar and vanilla extract until thoroughly combined, pale and light. Scrape down the sides of the bowl and then gradually add the beaten eggs, mixing well between each addition.

3. Sift the flour, ground almonds, cocoa powder, baking powder and salt into the bowl and mix until barely combined. Add the boiling water, scrape down the bowl and mix again for 30 seconds until the batter is silky smooth. Set aside while you quickly prepare the vanilla sponge mix.

MAKE THE VANILLA SPONGE MIX

4. In a clean bowl, cream the butter, caster sugar and vanilla extract until thoroughly combined, pale and light. Scrape down the sides of the bowl and gradually add the eggs, mixing well between each addition.

5. Sift the flour, cornflour, ground almonds, baking powder and salt into the bowl, add the milk and beat until smooth, mixing slowly at first to avoid the mixture spilling out of the bowl. Scrape down the bowl and mix again until the batter is silky smooth.

MARBLE THE CAKE MIXES AND BAKE THE CAKE

6. Use one tablespoon for the vanilla mix and a separate one for the chocolate mix and scoop alternate spoonfuls into the prepared tin, until all of the mixture has been used up and the tin is roughly half full. Tap the bottom of the tin sharply on the work surface to level it and then drag a round-bladed knife 4–5 times through the batter to swirl the chocolate and vanilla mixtures together. Tap again on the work surface to make sure the batter is level.

7. Bake for about 1 hour, until well risen, golden brown and a skewer inserted into the centre of the cake comes out clean. Leave to cool in the tin for 5 minutes and then turn out onto a wire rack and leave to cool completely.

DECORATE THE CAKE

8. Prepare the chocolate fudge frosting following the instructions on page 120, step 9.

9. Spoon the frosting over the top of the cake, allowing it to just drizzle over the sides. Arrange the malted chocolate balls all over the top and sprinkle chocolate pearls in between.

THE TRICK TO MARBLE CAKE IS NOT TO OVER-SWIRL THE TWO MIXTURES TOGETHER – LESS IS MORE!

IF THE FROSTING HAS SET TOO FIRM BY THE TIME YOU COME TO SPREAD IT, GENTLY WARM IT OVER A BOWL OF JUST-BOILED WATER.

SMALL BAKES

MALTED LAMINGTONS

MAKES 16

The success of these cakes relies on using sponge that is at least a day old. Older cake is easier to cut into neat squares and coat without the glaze becoming too crumby.

FOR THE VANILLA SPONGE

150g unsalted butter

150g caster sugar

1 teaspoon vanilla bean paste

3 eggs, lightly beaten

175g plain flour

3 tablespoons malted milk powder

2½ teaspoons baking powder

a good pinch of salt

2 tablespoons soured cream

2 tablespoons milk

FOR THE CHOCOLATE GLAZE

100g dark chocolate, chopped

75g milk chocolate

50g unsalted butter

225ml milk, warmed

2 tablespoons malted milk powder

350g icing sugar

50g cocoa powder

FOR THE FILLING AND COATING

16 teaspoons seedless raspberry jam

300g desiccated coconut

YOU WILL ALSO NEED

1 × 20cm square cake tin

disposable piping bag

MAKE THE VANILLA SPONGE

1. Preheat the oven to 180°C/160°C fan/gas mark 4. Butter and line the cake tin with buttered baking parchment.

2. Make the vanilla sponge mix following the instructions on page 17, up to the end of step 3, adding the malted milk powder with the dry ingredients and the soured cream with the milk.

3. Scoop the cake mix into the prepared tin and level with a palette knife or the back of a spoon. Bake for 25–30 minutes, until golden brown, well risen and a skewer inserted into the centre comes out clean. Leave to cool in the tin for 5 minutes, then turn out onto a wire rack. Leave until cold, wrap in cling film and set aside for 24 hours.

MAKE THE CHOCOLATE GLAZE

4. Melt all the chocolate and the butter in a heatproof bowl set over a pan of barely simmering water, making sure the bottom of the bowl doesn't touch the water. Stir until smooth, remove from the heat and cool slightly.

5. Warm the milk, in a small pan or in the microwave, until just below boiling. Add the malted milk powder and whisk until smooth. Leave to cool for 10 minutes.

6. Sift the icing sugar and cocoa into a large bowl, gradually add the warmed milk and mix to combine. Add the melted chocolate, mix until smooth and set aside for 30 minutes.

FILL AND COAT THE LAMINGTONS

7. Use a large serrated knife to cut the cake into squares. Spoon the jam into the piping bag and cut a 5mm hole in the end. Push the point of the piping bag into the side of each sponge and squeeze a blob of jam into the centre.

8. Spread half the desiccated coconut on a baking tray. Sit one of the sponges on the tines of a large dinner fork and dip it into the chocolate glaze to coat it, tapping the fork on the edge of the bowl to remove any excess, then roll in the desiccated coconut. Repeat with the remaining cakes, replacing the coconut halfway through when it gets too messy. Leave to set for at least 1 hour before serving.

JAM TARTS

MAKES 24

It's impossible to imagine a children's party without jam tarts. They have graced party tables for generations and are a fun and easy treat for kids to help bake. Use a selection of jam and curd flavours for a more delicious and colourful spread.

200g plain flour, plus extra for dusting

¼ teaspoon baking powder

a pinch of salt

125g unsalted butter, chilled and diced, plus extra for greasing

50g caster sugar

1 egg yolk

1–2 tablespoons ice-cold water

2 teaspoons lemon juice

16 teaspoons jam in 2 or 3 flavours

8 teaspoons lemon curd

YOU WILL ALSO NEED

2 x 12-hole bun tins

7½–8cm fluted round cutter

THIS RECIPE CAN EASILY BE DOUBLED IF YOU ARE FEEDING A LARGE CROWD OF REVELLERS!

1. Sift the flour, baking powder and salt into a mixing bowl. Add the butter and rub it in with your hands, lifting the mixture up and out of the bowl and gently pressing it between your fingertips as it drops back in. When there are only very small flecks of butter still visible, add the caster sugar and mix to combine.

2. Make a well in the middle of the dry ingredients and add the egg yolk, ice-cold water and lemon juice. Use a round-bladed butter knife to combine and, when the dough starts to clump together, use your hands to bring it into a ball. Knead very gently to combine, flatten into a disc, cover with cling film and chill for 1 hour. Grease the bun tins.

3. Roll out the chilled dough on a lightly dusted work surface to no more than 2mm thick. Use the cutter to stamp out discs and line the greased bun tins. Re-roll the offcuts to make more cases, then spoon a teaspoon of jam or lemon curd into each one. Chill again for 20 minutes. Preheat the oven to 180°C/160°C fan/gas mark 4.

4. Bake the tarts for 15–20 minutes, until the pastry is golden and the jam is bubbling. Cool in the tins for 20 minutes before transferring to a wire rack to cool completely.

PENGUINS ON ICE FLOES

MAKES 12

Make these cute fondant penguins the day before you plan to serve the cupcakes so that the fondant has plenty of time to dry out. You could also make them from marzipan. You will need a stand mixer or electric hand whisk to make the meringue.

FOR THE MERINGUES

100g caster sugar

2 egg whites

a pinch of salt

FOR THE FONDANT PENGUINS

350g white ready-roll fondant icing

black and yellow or orange food-colouring pastes

FOR THE CUPCAKES

175g unsalted butter

175g caster sugar

3 eggs, lightly beaten

1 teaspoon vanilla extract

200g plain flour

2 teaspoons baking powder

3 tablespoons milk

FOR THE VANILLA BUTTERCREAM

150g unsalted butter

300g icing sugar, plus extra for dusting

1 tablespoon milk

blue food-colouring paste

YOU WILL ALSO NEED

20 x 40cm baking sheet

small roasting tin

stand mixer or hand-held electric whisk

12-hole muffin tin

paper cases

MAKE THE MERINGUE

1. Preheat the oven to 200°C/180°C fan/gas mark 6 and line the baking sheet with baking parchment.

2. Spread the sugar over the roasting tin and heat in the oven for 4–5 minutes, or until hot to the touch. Lower the heat to 130°C/110°C fan/gas mark 1.

3. Meanwhile, tip the egg whites and salt into a large bowl or the bowl of a stand mixer and whisk on medium until they hold a soft peak when the whisks are lifted. Working quickly, tip the hot sugar into the bowl and continue to whisk on high for a further 8 minutes, until the meringue is very stiff, white and cold.

4. Use a palette knife to transfer the meringue to the prepared baking sheet and spread it out to a smooth, even layer roughly 3mm thick. Bake for about 1 hour, until firm and crisp, then turn off the oven and leave the meringue inside to cool down.

MAKE THE FONDANT PENGUINS

5. Break off 225g of the fondant icing and tint it black using the food-colouring paste. Divide it into 12 pieces. Take 1 piece, break off three-quarters of it and roll it into a penguin shape. Shape the smaller piece into wings and attach them to the body using a dab of cold water. Repeat to make 12 penguins.

6. On a clean work surface, divide 100g of the white icing into 12 equal pieces and then divide each piece into two, making one piece slightly larger than the other. Roll the pieces into balls and then press them into discs – the larger ones will be the penguin's tummies and the smaller ones the faces. Moisten with a little cold water and press onto the penguins.

7. Tint the remaining white icing yellow or orange and shape it into 24 feet and 12 beaks. Attach each to the penguins with a dab of water. Use black food-colouring paste to dot eyes onto the face of each penguin and leave them to set for at least 2 hours, or preferably overnight.

MAKE THE CUPCAKES

8. Preheat the oven to 180°C/160°C fan/gas mark 4 and line the muffin tins with paper cases.

9. Cream the butter with the caster sugar until really pale and light. Scrape down the sides of the bowl and mix again, then gradually add the beaten eggs along with the vanilla extract, mixing well between each addition. Sift the flour and baking powder into the bowl, add the milk and mix again until smooth.

10. Divide the mixture evenly between the cupcake cases and bake for about 20 minutes, until well risen, pale golden and a skewer inserted into the middle of the cakes comes out clean. Leave to cool in the tins for 2–3 minutes and then transfer to a wire rack to cool completely.

DECORATE THE CUPCAKES

11. Make the vanilla buttercream following the instructions on page 22 and tint it a very pale blue using food-colouring paste.

12. Spread the top of each cupcake with buttercream and then break the meringue into pieces and arrange them on top of the cupcakes. You may not need all of the meringue. Dust with icing sugar and sit a penguin on top of each meringue ice floe to serve.

FRANCES'S STAR BAKER MEDAL BISCUITS

MAKES 16–18

Everyone can be a star baker with these biscuit medals. Not only are they great fun to create, but they are the perfect party treat for everyone to enjoy. They can be used as edible party game prizes or given away in party bags as sweet keepsakes.

125g lightly salted butter
125g caster sugar
1 medium egg, lightly beaten
1 teaspoon vanilla extract
250g plain flour, plus extra for dusting
1 x tube hard butter toffee sweets, smashed into pieces
edible gold glitter

YOU WILL ALSO NEED
2 x baking sheets
8cm round cutter
6cm star cutter
5mm ribbon or decorative twine

1. In a large bowl, cream together the butter and sugar, then gradually beat in the egg and vanilla extract. Sift the flour into the bowl and mix to a fairly soft dough. Tip onto a lightly floured surface and knead gently, then wrap in cling film and chill for at least half an hour and up to 1 hour. Preheat the oven to 180°C/160°C fan/gas mark 4 and line the baking sheets with baking parchment.

2. Roll out the chilled dough on a lightly floured surface to about 5mm thick and use the 8cm round cutter to cut out as many discs as you can, re-rolling the scraps to make more biscuits. Use the star cutter to stamp out stars from the middle of each disc.

3. Carefully transfer the biscuits to the lined baking sheets, then push a skewer or the end of a paintbrush into the top of each biscuit to make a hole. Sprinkle the crushed sweets into the star spaces, directly onto the parchment, and bake for 10–15 minutes, until the sweets have melted and filled the stars and the biscuits are just golden around the edges.

4. While the biscuits are still warm, sprinkle edible glitter over the toffee stars and check the holes in the biscuits. If they have closed up during baking, gently open them up. Leave the biscuits to firm up on the trays until the melted sweets have completely set before transferring to a wire rack to cool completely.

5. Thread lengths of ribbon or twine through the holes in the biscuits, using the end of a skewer or a needle to help feed them through. Tie into loops and serve.

CAKE POPS

MAKES 20

A delicious and easy way to use up leftover cake and buttercream, cake pops can be decorated as elaborately as you like, but always with a good scattering of hundreds and thousands.

FOR THE POPS

75g dark chocolate, chopped
400g chocolate or vanilla sponge
200g vanilla buttercream, at room temperature (page 22)
a handful of crisp rice cereal

FOR THE DECORATION

200g dark chocolate, chopped
200g milk chocolate, chopped
50g white chocolate, chopped
assorted edible sprinkles
1–2 tablespoons popping candy, optional

YOU WILL ALSO NEED

20 x cake pop sticks
baking tray
disposable piping or freezer bag

MAKE THE POPS

1. Melt the chocolate in a heatproof bowl over a pan of barely simmering water, making sure the bottom of the bowl doesn't touch the water, or in the microwave on a low setting. Stir until smooth, remove from the heat and leave to cool for 20 minutes.

2. Break the cake into crumbs with your hands, tip it into a bowl, add the crisp rice cereal and mix well to combine.

3. In a separate bowl, mix the buttercream with the melted chocolate until smooth. Add the cake crumb mixture and mix again to combine thoroughly. Use clean hands to scrunch and bring the mixture together. Cover with cling film and chill for 30–60 minutes to firm up. Line the baking tray with baking parchment.

4. Using clean hands, roll the mixture into large bite-sized balls and arrange on the prepared baking tray. Press 1 cake pop stick into each ball, cover and chill for a further 30 minutes.

DECORATE THE POPS

5. Melt the dark chocolate using the method in step 1. Stir until smooth, remove from the heat and leave to cool for a few minutes. Repeat with the milk chocolate.

6. Dip half the cake pops into the melted dark chocolate to coat, allowing any excess to drip back into the bowl, and return to the baking tray. Repeat to coat the rest of the cake pops in milk chocolate.

7. Melt the white chocolate, scoop it into a disposable piping bag or a freezer bag, twist the end to seal and snip to a fine point. Drizzle the white chocolate in a haphazard fashion over each cake pop. Scatter with sprinkles and popping candy, if using, and leave for at least 30 minutes to set before serving.

MINI BERRY CAKES

MAKES 24

Pretty bite-sized cakes filled with a secret centre of raspberry or blackberry purée and topped with buttercream flavoured with fresh fruit. Perfect for little hands!

FOR THE CUPCAKES

175g unsalted butter

175g caster sugar

3 eggs, lightly beaten

1 teaspoon vanilla extract

200g plain flour

2 teaspoons baking powder

3 tablespoons milk

FOR THE BERRY BUTTERCREAMS

200g unsalted butter

400g icing sugar, plus extra for dusting

1 teaspoon vanilla extract

1 tablespoon milk

300g raspberries

300g blackberries or blueberries

juice of ½ lemon

2 tablespoons caster sugar

YOU WILL ALSO NEED

2 x 12-hole mini fairy cake tins

24 mini fairy cake cases

2 x disposable piping bags

2 x medium open star nozzles

MAKE THE CUPCAKES

1. Preheat the oven to 180°C/160°C fan/gas mark 4 and position the shelves as close to the middle as possible, leaving enough space between them for the cakes to rise. Line the tins with the paper cases.

2. In a large bowl or the bowl of a stand mixer, cream the butter with the caster sugar until really pale and light. Scrape down the sides of the bowl and mix again.

3. Gradually add the beaten eggs and vanilla extract, mixing well between each addition. Sift the flour and baking powder into the bowl, add the milk and mix until smooth.

4. Divide the cake mix evenly between the paper cases and bake for 12–15 minutes, until well risen, pale golden and a skewer inserted into the centre of the cakes comes out clean. Leave to cool in the tins for 2–3 minutes and then transfer to a wire rack and leave until completely cold.

ICE WITH THE BERRY BUTTERCREAMS

5. Make a vanilla buttercream following the instructions on page 22. Divide between 2 bowls, cover and set aside.

6. Tip 250g of the raspberries into a small saucepan with a squeeze of lemon juice and 1 tablespoon of caster sugar. Place over a low-medium heat and cook, stirring frequently, until the berries have broken down to a soft jammy consistency. Remove from the heat, press through a sieve into a clean bowl and leave until cold. Repeat with 250g of the blackberries or blueberries.

7. Use a small sharp knife to cut a small sponge cone from the top of each cupcake. Fill the holes of half of the cakes with a teaspoonful of raspberry purée and the other half with the blackberry or blueberry purée.

8. Mix the remaining raspberry purée into one bowl of buttercream, and the blackberry or blueberry purée into the other. Spoon one of the buttercreams into a piping bag fitted with an open star nozzle and pipe a swirl on top of the corresponding cakes. Spoon the second buttercream into another bag and pipe rosettes over the remaining cakes. Top each cake with a fresh berry and dust with icing sugar to serve.

DOUGHNUT RINGS & HOLES

Fresh home-cooked doughnuts are irresistible and even more so when dipped in sugar and topped with fresh raspberry, lemon or chocolate glaze. For best results you will need a sugar thermometer to check the temperature of the cooking oil.

FOR THE DOUGHNUTS

450g strong white bread flour, plus extra for dusting

325g caster sugar

7g fast-action yeast

a pinch of salt

200–225ml whole milk, warm

1 egg, plus 1 yolk

75g unsalted butter, diced

1 litre sunflower oil, for deep-frying

FOR THE CHOCOLATE GLAZE

125g dark chocolate, chopped

80g milk chocolate, chopped

20g unsalted butter

100ml whipping cream

1 tablespoon golden syrup

FOR THE RASPBERRY ICING

200g raspberries

freshly squeezed juice of 1 lemon

400g icing sugar

YOU WILL ALSO NEED

1 x 6–7cm round cutter

1 x 3cm round cutter

2 x baking trays

sugar thermometer

PREPARE THE DOUGH

1. Tip the flour, 75g of the sugar, the yeast and the salt into a large bowl or the bowl of a stand mixer fitted with the dough hook. Make a well in the centre of the dry ingredients, add the warm milk, whole egg, egg yolk and butter. If using a machine, mix steadily for about 5 minutes, until the dough is smooth and elastic. It will still be slightly sticky. Scrape the dough out of the bowl onto a lightly dusted work surface and knead with your hands for 1 minute. If making the doughnuts by hand, combine all the ingredients in the bowl and then turn out onto a lightly floured work surface and use slightly wet hands to knead for 5–10 minutes, until silky smooth and elastic.

2. Shape the dough into a smooth ball and place it in a large, lightly oiled mixing bowl. Cover with cling film and leave to prove in a warm, draught-free place for about 1 hour, or until the dough has doubled in size. Lightly oil the baking trays.

3. Tip the proved dough onto a lightly dusted work surface and knead very gently for 30 seconds. Roll it out to just over 1cm thick and use the large cutter to stamp out discs. Use the smaller cutter to stamp out holes from the middle of each doughnut. Arrange on the prepared baking trays, leaving plenty of space between them, cover loosely with oiled cling film and leave to rise again for 40–45 minutes.

MAKE THE CHOCOLATE GLAZE AND RASPBERRY ICING

4. Melt all the ingredients for the chocolate glaze together in a small pan over a low heat, stirring constantly until smooth. Remove from the heat and cool slightly.

5. Tip the raspberries into a small bowl and add a drop of the lemon juice and a teaspoon of the icing sugar. Crush the berries with a fork and leave for 20 minutes to become very juicy. Strain the juice into a clean bowl and discard the solids left in the sieve.

6. Mix the raspberry juice with half the remaining icing sugar to make a smooth but slightly runny glaze. Mix the remaining icing sugar with the lemon juice to make a smooth, drizzly icing.

COOK AND COAT THE DOUGHNUTS

6. Pour the sunflower oil into a large, shallow saucepan so that it comes at least halfway up the sides of the pan. Pop a thermometer into the oil and heat to 180–185°C.

7. Carefully drop 3–4 doughnut rings or holes at a time into the hot oil and fry for 1–2 minutes on each side, turning them over after the first 20 seconds to prevent large air pockets forming on the top. They are ready when they are golden brown all over. Remove from the oil with a slotted spoon and drain thoroughly on kitchen paper. Make sure the oil comes back up to temperature before adding the next batch of doughnuts.

8. Spread out the remaining caster sugar on a clean baking tray and lay the warm doughnuts in it to coat the bottom halves. Remove from the sugar and arrange, sugar side down, on a wire rack.

9. While still warm, dip the tops of one-third of the doughnuts in the raspberry icing and one-third in the lemon icing. Spoon the chocolate glaze into a disposable piping bag or freezer bag, snip the end to a point and drizzle the glaze over the remaining doughnuts.

COOK EACH DOUGHNUT FOR ABOUT 20 SECONDS BEFORE FLIPPING IT OVER TO PREVENT ANY LARGE AIR POCKETS FORMING THAT WOULD MAKE IT HARDER TO FLIP THEM LATER.

MILKSHAKE CUPCAKES

MAKES 12

*Look out for pretty paper drinking straws in bright or pastel colours to complete
the milkshake theme for these cakes. This recipe uses strawberry milkshake
powder but you could also use banana or chocolate, whichever you prefer.*

FOR THE CUPCAKES

175g unsalted butter

125g caster sugar

3 eggs, lightly beaten

1 teaspoon vanilla extract

200g plain flour

2 teaspoons baking powder

75g strawberry milkshake powder

3 tablespoons milk

FOR THE MILKSHAKE BUTTERCREAM

150g unsalted butter

250g icing sugar

50g strawberry milkshake powder

1 teaspoon vanilla extract

2–3 tablespoons milk

pink and white sprinkles

YOU WILL ALSO NEED

1 x 12-hole muffin tin

paper cases

pretty paper straws

1. Preheat the oven to 180°C/160°C fan/gas mark 4
and line the muffin tin with paper cases.

2. Cream the butter with the caster sugar until very pale
and light. Scrape down the sides of the bowl and mix again.
Gradually add the eggs along with the vanilla extract,
mixing well between each addition.

3. Sift the flour and baking powder into the bowl, add
the milkshake powder and milk and mix again until smooth.
Divide evenly between the paper cases and bake for about
20 minutes, until well risen, pale golden and a skewer
inserted into the middle of the cakes comes out clean.
Leave to cool in the tins for 2–3 minutes and then transfer
to a wire rack to cool completely.

4. Prepare the buttercream following the instructions
on page 22, adding the milkshake powder along with
the icing sugar.

5. Use a palette knife to spread the top of each cupcake
with a generous amount of buttercream. Scatter sprinkles
round the edges and press straws into each cake to serve.

ICED GEMS

MAKES 100

As this recipe makes so many tiny little biscuits you could pop a few into each party bag to take home after the party.

FOR THE BISCUITS

200g plain flour, plus extra for dusting
½ teaspoon baking powder
a pinch of salt
100g unsalted butter, chilled and diced
75g icing sugar
1 egg
1 teaspoon vanilla extract

FOR THE ICING

500g royal icing sugar
assorted food-colouring pastes
edible sugar balls or pearls

YOU WILL ALSO NEED

3cm round cutter
2–3 baking sheets
disposable piping bag
small open star nozzles

MAKE THE BISCUITS

1. Sift the flour, baking powder and salt into a large mixing bowl, add the chilled diced butter and use a butter or palette knife to cut the butter into the dry ingredients. Once the butter is partially incorporated, use your hands to finish rubbing it into the flour. When there are only very small flecks of butter remaining, sift the icing sugar into the bowl and mix to combine with a spoon or palette knife.

2. In a small bowl, beat the egg with the vanilla. Make a well in the centre of the dry ingredients, add the egg mixture and mix to combine using the palette knife. Gather the dough into a smooth ball with your hands, flatten it into a disc and wrap it in cling film. Chill for 1 hour. Line the baking sheets with parchment paper.

3. Lightly dust the work surface with flour and roll out the dough to 2–3mm thick. Dust the cookie cutter in flour to prevent it sticking and stamp out small biscuits from the rolled out dough, re-rolling the trimmings to make more. You may need to dust the cutter more than once. Arrange the biscuits on the prepared baking sheets and chill for a further 30 minutes. Preheat the oven to 180°C/160°C fan/gas mark 4.

4. Bake the biscuits in batches for about 12 minutes, or until crisp and light golden brown. Leave to cool on the baking sheets.

ICE THE GEMS

5. Tip the royal icing sugar into a mixing bowl and, whisking continuously, gradually add enough cold water to make a smooth, thick paste that will hold a very firm ribbon trail.

6. Divide the icing into 3 or 4 bowls and tint each one a different colour using cocktail sticks dipped in the different food-colouring pastes. Spoon the icing into disposable piping bags fitted with open star nozzles and pipe a single rosette of icing onto each biscuit. Top each rosette with a sugar ball or pearl and then leave for at least 2 hours to harden before serving.

LEMON SPRINKLE CAKES

MAKES 10–12

For best results when making funfetti cakes or bakes, look out for brightly coloured sprinkles that are very lightly coated with a wax seal. This will ensure that the colours remain bright after baking and that the sprinkles don't simply melt into the cake mix. Silicone Bundt tins are easy to use as they don't require greasing. They are available online or in good bakeware shops.

FOR THE CAKES

150g unsalted butter

150g caster sugar

2 eggs, lightly beaten, plus 2 egg whites

125g plain flour

25g cornflour

2 teaspoons baking powder

2 tablespoons milk

finely grated zest of 1 unwaxed lemon

2–3 tablespoons brightly coloured jimmies sprinkles

FOR THE GLAZE

2 tablespoons freshly squeezed lemon juice

150g icing sugar, sifted

extra sprinkles, to decorate

YOU WILL ALSO NEED

1 x 12-hole silicone or metal mini Bundt tin

large disposable piping bag

1. Preheat the oven to 180°C/160°C fan/gas mark 4. If you're using metal tins, brush them with melted butter and dust with plain flour.

2. Cream the butter with the caster sugar until pale and light. Scrape down the sides of the mixing bowl and gradually add the lightly beaten eggs, mixing well between each addition. Sift the flour, cornflour and baking powder into the bowl, add the milk and lemon zest and mix again to combine.

3. In a separate bowl, whisk the egg whites until they hold stiff peaks when you lift the whisk away. Using a large metal spoon or rubber spatula, fold the sprinkles into the cake mix, followed by the beaten egg whites.

4. Working quickly but gently, so as not to knock out any air from the mix, scoop the batter into the piping bag and fill the tins evenly – you will only need to half-fill each hole. Bake for 15–20 minutes, until well risen and golden brown. Leave to cool in the tins for 1–2 minutes and then carefully turn out onto a wire rack and leave until cold.

5. If the cakes have domed bottoms, use a serrated knife to trim them flat and then place all the cakes on a wire rack set over a tray to catch any dribbles.

6. In a small bowl, whisk the lemon juice with the icing sugar to make a smooth and drizzly icing. Carefully spoon the icing over each cake, letting it dribble down the sides. Scatter with sprinkles and leave to set for 1 hour before serving.

THE EASIEST AND QUICKEST WAY TO FILL MINI BUNDT TINS WITH CAKE MIX IS TO USE A PIPING BAG.

PIRATE SHIP CUPCAKES

MAKES 12

Shiver me timbers! Pirate themes are always popular at parties and this simple and fun cupcake idea is as much about craft as it is about baking. You can make the sails in advance so that they're ready to go on the day.

FOR THE CUPCAKES

175g unsalted butter

175g caster sugar

3 eggs, lightly beaten

1 teaspoon vanilla extract

200g plain flour

2 teaspoons baking powder

3 tablespoons milk

FOR THE GINGERBREAD BISCUITS

125g plain flour, plus extra for dusting

1 teaspoon ground ginger

1 teaspoon ground cinnamon

¼ teaspoon baking powder

a large pinch of salt

75g unsalted butter, chilled and diced

50g caster sugar

1 egg yolk

1 rounded tablespoon golden syrup

FOR THE BUTTERCREAM

250g unsalted butter

500g icing sugar, sifted

2 teaspoons vanilla extract

2 tablespoons milk

FOR THE DECORATION

200g ready-roll brown fondant or sugarpaste icing

1 tablespoon seedless raspberry or apricot jam

125g royal icing sugar, plus extra for dusting

brown and blue food-colouring pastes

YOU WILL ALSO NEED

1 x 12-hole muffin tin

black or brown paper cupcake cases

baking sheet

Pirate ship template, page 14

blue and white striped paper

red and white striped paper

hole punch

12 x wooden skewers or cake pop sticks

12 x small paper skull-and-cross-bone pennants

2 x disposable piping bags

MAKE THE CUPCAKES

1. Preheat the oven to 180°C/160°C fan/gas mark 4 and position the shelf in the middle. Line the muffin tin with paper cases.

2. In a large bowl or the bowl of a stand mixer, cream the butter with the caster sugar until really pale and light. Scrape down the sides of the bowl and mix again.

3. Gradually add the beaten eggs and vanilla extract, mixing well between each addition. Sift the flour and baking powder into the bowl, add the milk and mix again until smooth.

4. Divide the cake mix evenly between the cupcake cases and bake for about 20 minutes until well risen, pale golden and a skewer inserted into the centre of the cakes comes out clean. Leave to cool in the tins for 2–3 minutes and then transfer to a wire rack to cool completely.

MAKE THE GINGERBREAD BOATS

5. Sift the flour, ginger, cinnamon, baking powder and salt into a large mixing bowl. Add the butter and rub it in using your fingers, lifting the mixture up and out of the bowl and gently pressing it between your fingertips as it drops back in. When there are no visible flecks of butter remaining, add the caster sugar and mix again to combine.

6. In a small bowl, mix together the egg yolk and golden syrup and pour this into the biscuit mix. Bring the dough together into a ball, flatten it into a disc and wrap it in cling film. Chill for about 1 hour, or until firm. Line the baking sheet with parchment paper.

7. Roll out the dough on a lightly dusted work surface to 2–3mm thick. Use the template on page 14 to cut out 15 boats – you will only need 12 but it's good to have some spares. Place on the prepared baking sheet and chill for 20 minutes. Preheat the oven to 180°C/160°C fan/gas mark 4.

8. Bake the biscuits for about 12 minutes, until firm and starting to darken slightly at the edges. Leave to cool on the baking sheets.

MAKE THE PAPER SAILS

9. Cut the striped paper into 4 x 6–7 cm strips – you will need 2 for each cake. Use a hole punch to stamp 2 holes in the centre of each strip, one at the top and one at the bottom. Thread 2 paper strips through a cake pop stick to create a billowing sail effect. Secure a skull-and-cross-bone pennant to the top of each mast using a little sticky tape.

DECORATE THE CUPCAKES

10. Roll out the brown fondant or sugarpaste on a lightly dusted work surface to 1–2mm thick. Use the template to cut out 15 boat shapes, re-rolling the offcuts if needed to make enough shapes. Warm a little jam in a small pan or in the microwave and lightly brush the tops of the boat biscuits. Lay a fondant boat shape on top of each one and press neatly into place.

11. Prepare the royal icing following the instructions on page 21 to make a stiff writing icing that will hold a firm ribbon trail when the whisk is lifted from the bowl. Tint the icing brown using food-colouring paste and scoop it into a disposable piping bag – it should be a lighter brown than the fondant icing. Snip the end of the bag to a fine point and pipe an outline and wooden details onto each boat, using the detailed instructions on page 21 as a guide. Leave to dry for at least 30 minutes.

12. Meanwhile, make the vanilla buttercream following the instructions on page 22. Add blue food-colouring paste and stir with a palette knife to make a swirly, marbled pale blue icing. Spread roughly in waves on top of each cupcake.

13. Push a mast and sails into each cupcake and press a boat biscuit into the buttercream in front of each one so that it rests against the mast.

CATHRYN'S MOUSTACHE-POP BISCUITS

MAKES 16 LARGE MOUSTACHES

These are simply yummy fun on a stick. Take a selfie, do an impression or just gobble up your chocolatey moustache! If you don't fancy being a brunette, make a blonde caramel biscuit or a spicy red ginger moustache instead.

250g unsalted butter, very soft

100g icing sugar

2 tablespoons custard powder or cornflour

200g plain flour

50g cocoa powder

a big pinch of salt

1 egg, beaten

YOU WILL ALSO NEED

2 or 3 baking sheets

piping bag

star nozzle

lolly sticks

1. Preheat the oven to 200°C/180°C fan/gas mark 6 and position the shelf as close to the middle as possible. Line the baking sheets with baking parchment.

2. Tip all the ingredients into a food-processor and blitz for 20 seconds. Scrape down the sides of the bowl and blitz again to make a smooth mixture. Alternatively, cream the butter, icing sugar and custard powder in a mixing bowl until smooth and pale, add the flour, cocoa and salt and mix. Add the egg and combine until you have a smooth mixture.

3. Fit the piping bag with the star nozzle and fill it with the biscuit dough. Squeeze a generous blob onto the baking parchment and then pipe outwards to make a curly moustache shape. Pipe another blob next to, and touching, the first one and pipe the other side of the moustache. Gently push a lolly stick into one end and repeat until the mixture is used up.

4. Bake for around 12 minutes, until the moustaches feel firmish to the touch. Leave to cool on the tray for 5–10 minutes to properly firm up, then transfer to a wire rack to cool completely.

TO MAKE CARAMEL MOUSTACHES

Replace the cocoa powder with 50g more flour and add 1 teaspoon caramel flavouring.

TO MAKE GINGER MOUSTACHES

Replace the cocoa powder with 50g more flour and add 2 teaspoons ground cinnamon and 1 teaspoon ground ginger.

NUMBER COOKIES

MAKES 20–24

For these cookies you will need either small number-shaped cookie cutters or a steady hand to draw the number outlines. You could also use small letter cutters in place of the numbers and spell out the birthday girl or boy's name.

FOR THE COOKIE DOUGH

225g unsalted butter
150g icing sugar
1 egg, lightly beaten
grated zest of ½ unwaxed lemon
1 teaspoon vanilla bean paste
350g plain flour, plus extra for dusting
a pinch of salt

FOR THE DECORATION

500g royal icing sugar
2 x pastel food-colouring pastes
assorted nonpareils sprinkles

YOU WILL ALSO NEED

2 x baking sheets
8cm round cutter
small number cutters
2 x disposable piping bags

MAKE THE COOKIES

1. In a large bowl or the bowl of a stand mixer, cream the butter and icing sugar until pale, light and fluffy. Scrape down the sides of the bowl and gradually add the beaten egg, mixing well until smooth. Add the lemon zest and vanilla bean paste and mix again.

2. Sift the flour and salt into the bowl and mix until smooth. Shape into a disc, wrap in cling film and chill for 2 hours until firm. Line the baking sheets with baking parchment.

3. Roll out the cookie dough on a lightly dusted work surface to 2–3mm thick. Use the round cutter to stamp out discs and arrange them on the prepared baking sheets. Re-roll the offcuts to make more cookies. Chill for 20 minutes. Preheat the oven to 180°C/160°C fan/gas mark 4.

4. Take the cookies out of the fridge and press numbers into the centres using the number cutters, stamping halfway through each cookie, but not all the way through to the other side. Bake for 10–12 minutes, until pale golden. Leave to cool on the baking sheets until firm before carefully transferring to a wire rack to cool completely.

DECORATE THE COOKIES

5. Sift the royal icing sugar into a bowl and gradually add 75–100ml water to make a smooth but thick writing icing. It should be thick enough to hold a firm ribbon trail when the spoon or whisk is lifted from the bowl (see page 21).

6. Spoon 3 tablespoons of the icing into a piping bag and snip the point to a fine writing nozzle. Cover the rest of the icing in cling film. Pipe a white line around the outside edge of each biscuit and outline each of the numbers. Leave to dry for 30 minutes. Spread the nonpareils sprinkles onto a small plate.

7. Spoon 3 tablespoons of icing into a bowl and tint it a pale pastel shade. Add a drop of water to make the icing very slightly runnier. Spoon this into a second piping bag and snip the end to a fine point. Fill the number of each biscuit with icing and then hold the biscuit horizontally, iced side down, and dip it into the sprinkles to coat the numbers; the sprinkles shouldn't stick to the rest of the dry biscuit. Leave to dry for 20 minutes.

8. Tint the remaining icing a contrasting pastel shade and add a drop of water to loosen it. Use a teaspoon to carefully flood the space around each number with icing. Leave to set for at least 1 hour before serving.

BEE & LADYBIRD CUPCAKES

MAKES 12

These are possibly the easiest decorative cakes to make as they require neither specialist equipment nor a lot of skill. Any trimmings from the tops of the cakes can be used to make cake pops or mini trifles.

FOR THE CUPCAKES

175g unsalted butter

175g caster sugar

3 eggs, lightly beaten

1 teaspoon vanilla extract

200g plain flour

2 teaspoons baking powder

3 tablespoons milk

FOR THE VANILLA BUTTERCREAM

150g unsalted butter

300g icing sugar, plus extra for dusting

1 teaspoon vanilla extract

1 tablespoon milk

FOR THE DECORATION

150g ready-roll yellow fondant icing

150g ready-roll black fondant icing

150g ready-roll red fondant icing

12 giant white chocolate buttons

1 x tube black writing icing

1 x tube white writing icing

thin black liquorice

YOU WILL ALSO NEED

1 x 12-hole muffin tin

paper cupcake cases

plain round cutters the same size as the top edge

of the cupcake cases

MAKE THE CUPCAKES

1. Preheat the oven to 180°C/160°C fan/gas mark 4 and position the shelf in the middle. Line the muffin tin with paper cases.

2. In a large bowl or the bowl of a stand mixer, cream the butter with the caster sugar until really pale and light. Scrape down the sides of the bowl and mix again.

3. Gradually add the beaten eggs and vanilla extract, mixing well between each addition. Sift the flour and baking powder into the bowl, add the milk and mix again until smooth.

4. Divide the cake mix evenly between the cupcake cases and bake for about 20 minutes, until well risen, pale golden and a skewer inserted into the centre of the cakes comes out clean. Leave to cool in the tins for 2—3 minutes and then transfer to a wire rack to cool completely.

5. Meanwhile, make the vanilla buttercream following the instructions on page 22. If the cupcakes have domed in the oven, use a serrated knife to level the top of each cake. Use a palette knife to cover the top of each cake in a smooth layer of buttercream.

DECORATE THE BEES

6. Roll out the yellow fondant on a lightly dusted work surface to 2mm thick. Use a plain round cutter to stamp out 6 discs and carefully cover 6 of the cupcakes.

7. Roll out half the black fondant to 2mm thick and stamp out 3 more discs. Cut each one into 6 horizontal slices and lightly brush with a little cold water. Position 3 black strips evenly apart on one half of the top of each yellow cupcake.

8. Press 2 white chocolate drops into the top of each cake to make wings and use the tubes of black and white writing icing to pipe eyes and mouths. Cut the liquorice into 2–3cm-long slivers and use a skewer to push 2 into each cupcake for antennae.

DECORATE THE LADYBIRDS

9. Roll out the red fondant to 2mm thick and stamp out 6 discs. Use these to cover the remaining cupcakes.

10. Roll out the remaining black fondant as before and cut out another 3 discs. Cut each one in half, lightly brush with cold water and stick one semicircle onto each red cupcake.

11. Use the blunt edge of a large knife to press a dividing line into the red icing where the wing cases would meet. Roll up scraps of black icing to make spots, flattening them into 5–10mm discs. Brush with cold water and stick 6 or 8 spots onto each ladybird. Pipe eyes using the writing icing and leave to set for 30 minutes before serving.

S'MORES CUPCAKES

MAKES 12

These rich little cakes are best suited to older children (or adults!), who will love something a little more grown up for their party table. It's tricky, though not impossible, to make marshmallow without a stand mixer, but you'll need a good hand-held electric whisk or lots of stamina!

FOR THE CUPCAKES

12 digestive biscuits, crumbled into chunks

200g caster sugar

175g plain flour

1½ teaspoons baking powder

½ teaspoon bicarbonate of soda

a pinch of salt

100ml sunflower oil

2 eggs

2 tablespoons soured cream

50g cocoa powder

125ml boiling water

FOR THE MARSHMALLOW TOPPING

1 leaf platinum-grade leaf gelatine

200g caster sugar

2 egg whites

1 teaspoon vanilla bean paste

a pinch of salt

FOR THE CHOCOLATE GLAZE

100g dark chocolate, chopped, plus 50g snapped into squares

40g milk chocolate, chopped

100ml double cream

1 tablespoon golden syrup

a pinch of salt

YOU WILL ALSO NEED

1 x 12-hole muffin tin

paper cupcake cases

stand mixer fitted with the whisk attachment, or a good hand-held whisk

large piping bag

plain 1cm nozzle

cook's blowtorch, optional

MAKE THE CUPCAKES

1. Preheat the oven to 180°C/160°C fan/gas mark 4 and line the muffin tin with paper cases.

2. Scatter half the digestive chunks between the cupcake cases.

3. Sift the caster sugar, flour, baking powder, bicarbonate of soda and salt into a large mixing bowl. Add the sunflower oil, eggs and soured cream and beat until smooth. In a separate bowl, whisk the cocoa powder and boiling water to a smooth paste. Add this to the cake mixture and beat again until silky smooth.

4. Divide the cake mix evenly between the cupcake cases, covering the digestive chunks as you do so, and bake for 20–25 minutes until well risen and a skewer inserted into the centre of the cakes comes out clean. Leave to cool in the tin for 5 minutes and then transfer to a wire rack and leave until cold.

MAKE THE MARSHMALLOW TOPPING

5. In a large heatproof bowl, soak the gelatine leaf in 2 tablespoons of cold water until soft and floppy – this will take about 10 minutes.

6. Meanwhile, place the caster sugar, egg whites, vanilla bean paste and salt into a separate heatproof bowl and set it over a pan of simmering water, making sure the bottom of the bowl doesn't touch the water. Whisk constantly with a balloon whisk for about 5 minutes, until the sugar has dissolved, the meringue is hot to the touch and the mixture holds a firm ribbon trail when the whisk is lifted.

7. Take the bowl off the pan and swap it with the bowl containing the softened gelatine and water. Allow the gelatine to melt in the water for 30–60 seconds and then tip the contents into the meringue mix. Return this bowl to the pan and continue cooking for 1 minute, then spoon the meringue into the bowl of a stand mixer. Whisk on high for about 3 minutes, until the marshmallow has cooled and thickened enough to hold a soft peak when you lift the whisks. You can do this step using a good hand-held electric whisk, but it will take longer.

8. Use a rubber spatula to scoop the marshmallow into the piping bag fitted with the nozzle and pipe a generous mound on top of each cold cupcake. Leave in a cool place for about 1 hour to set.

MAKE THE CHOCOLATE GLAZE

9. Melt the 100g chopped dark chocolate with the milk chocolate, double cream, golden syrup and salt in a heatproof bowl over a pan of barely simmering water, making sure the bottom of the bowl doesn't touch the water. Stir until smooth and leave to cool slightly.

10. Use a blowtorch, if you have one, to lightly scorch the marshmallows, being careful not to set the cupcake cases alight.

11. Spoon a little chocolate glaze over the top of each marshmallow, scatter with the reserved biscuit crumbs and press a square of chocolate into the top of each cake to serve.

IF THE CUPCAKES RISE UNEVENLY OR HAVE DOMED TOPS AFTER BAKING, USE A SERRATED KNIFE TO SLICE OFF THE TOPS TO EVEN THEM UP AND MAKE THEM LEVEL BEFORE FROSTING

MERINGUE KISSES

MAKES ABOUT 40

You will need to use food-colouring pastes rather than liquid colours for these bite-sized mini meringues. For extra pizazz try sprinkling each meringue with sprinkles or hundreds and thousands just before baking.

200g caster sugar
100g egg whites (from about 3 large eggs)
a pinch of salt
assorted food-colouring pastes

YOU WILL ALSO NEED
2 × large baking sheets
a small roasting tin
stand mixer fitted with a whisk attachment,
or hand-held electric whisk
craft brush
3 × disposable piping bags
1cm star or plain nozzles

1. Preheat the oven to 200°C/180°C fan/gas mark 6 and line the baking sheets with baking parchment.

2. Spread the sugar over the roasting tin and heat in the oven for 4–5 minutes, or until hot to the touch. Lower the heat to 130°C/110°C fan/gas mark 1.

3. Meanwhile, tip the egg whites and salt into a large bowl or the bowl of a stand mixer and whisk on medium until they hold a soft peak when the whisks are lifted. Working quickly, tip the hot sugar into the bowl and continue to whisk on high for a further 8 minutes, until the meringue is very stiff, white and cold.

4. Fit one of the piping bags with the nozzle and then take one of the food-colouring pastes and use the brush to paint 3 evenly spaced stripes on the inside, from the nozzle towards the opening. Carefully fill the bag with one-third of the meringue mixture and pipe 3–4cm meringues onto the prepared baking sheet in the shape of small kisses, rosettes or spirals. Repeat with the remaining meringue, painting different colours, or combinations of colours, in each bag.

5. Bake the meringues for about 40 minutes, swapping the trays around halfway through to make sure they bake evenly. Remove from the oven and leave to cool completely on the trays.

BLUEBERRY BAKEWELL SLICES

MAKES 20

You could ice these slices with a lemon glace icing if you like and scatter with toasted almonds after baking, but not before.

FOR THE SHORTBREAD BASE

100g plain flour

a pinch of salt

75g unsalted butter, chilled and diced

25g icing sugar

FOR THE BAKEWELL TOPPING

2 heaped tablespoons blueberry jam or lemon curd

150g unsalted butter

150g caster sugar

3 eggs, lightly beaten

100g ground almonds

50g plain flour

½ teaspoon baking powder

a pinch of salt

finely grated zest of 1 unwaxed lemon

1 tablespoon milk

200g blueberries

1 tablespoon flaked almonds

YOU WILL ALSO NEED

20 x 30cm baking tin

MAKE THE SHORTBREAD BASE

1. Preheat the oven to 180°C/160°C fan/gas mark 4. Butter the tin and line the base and sides with baking parchment.

2. Tip the flour and salt into a mixing bowl, add the butter and cut it into the flour using a round-bladed knife, then switch to your hands to rub the butter into the flour until there are only very small flecks of butter still visible. Sift the icing sugar into the bowl and mix again with your hands until combined.

3. Tip the mixture into the prepared tin and use your hands to press it into a firm, even layer covering the base of the tin. Bake for about 20 minutes until biscuity and golden brown at the edges. Leave to cool for 20 minutes.

MAKE THE TOPPING AND ASSEMBLE THE LAYERS

4. Spread the jam or lemon curd over the shortbread base.

5. Cream the butter with the caster sugar until pale and light, then gradually add the beaten eggs, mixing well between each addition and scraping down the sides of the bowl from time to time.

6. Sift the ground almonds, flour, baking powder and salt into the bowl, add the lemon zest and milk and mix again until smooth and all the ingredients are thoroughly combined. Fold the blueberries into the batter using a spatula or large metal spoon.

7. Carefully spoon the topping over the base layer and spread it to an even layer with a palette knife or the back of a spoon. Scatter with flaked almonds and bake for 30–35 minutes until set, risen and golden brown. Leave to cool completely before cutting into fingers to serve.

RICHARD'S FUNFETTI SHORTBREAD SANDWICH BISCUITS

MAKES 25 SANDWICHES

These biscuits are always a real winner in our house and they make excellent dunkers! They are quick to make, colourful, and the little 'uns can even get stuck in pressing out the shapes.

FOR THE BISCUITS

300g plain flour, plus extra for dusting
2½ tablespoons coloured jimmies sprinkles
200g unsalted butter
100g caster sugar
½ teaspoon vanilla paste or extract
1 egg yolk
½ teaspoon salt

FOR THE BUTTERCREAM

75g unsalted butter
150g icing sugar
½ teaspoon vanilla paste or extract
pink food colouring

YOU WILL ALSO NEED

baking sheet
5cm fluted or round cutter
piping bag

MAKE THE BISCUITS

1. Line the baking sheet with baking parchment. Measure the flour into a bowl and mix in the sprinkles.

2. In a separate bowl, cream the butter. Add the sugar, vanilla, egg yolk and salt and beat together until soft and creamy. Add the sprinkle flour and mix to combine, then tip onto a lightly floured surface and knead gently until fully combined, handling the dough as little as possible.

3. Lay the dough between 2 sheets of baking parchment and roll out to 5mm thick – you may need to turn the parchment over, peel it off and re-lay it to prevent kinks. Stamp out discs, re-rolling the scraps as necessary. Transfer to the prepared baking sheet and chill for 20 minutes. Preheat the oven to 180°C/160°C fan/gas mark 4.

4. Bake the biscuits for 12–14 minutes, until just beginning to colour. Leave to cool on a wire rack.

MAKE THE BUTTERCREAM AND FILL THE SANDWICHES

5. Beat together the butter, icing sugar, vanilla and a small amount of pink food colouring until creamy.

6. When the biscuits are completely cold, fill the piping bag with the buttercream and snip a small opening in the end. Lay half the biscuits flat side up and pipe spirals of buttercream onto them, working from the outsides in. Gently sandwich with the rest of the biscuits and leave to set for at least 1 hour and ideally overnight.

CHOCOLATE SWISS ROLL SLICES

MAKES 12

Timing is everything when it comes to baking this cake – a minute over and it will be tricky to roll as the cake may crack – so be sure to set a timer! The buttercream will be slightly softer than that used for other cakes as this will make it easier to spread over the delicate sponge.

FOR THE CHOCOLATE SPONGE

75g caster sugar

3 eggs

1 teaspoon vanilla bean paste or extract

75g plain flour

25g cocoa powder

½ teaspoon baking powder

a pinch of salt

25g unsalted butter, melted and cooled slightly

FOR THE VANILLA BUTTERCREAM

100g unsalted butter

200g icing sugar, sifted

1 teaspoon vanilla bean paste

2 tablespoons milk

FOR THE CHOCOLATE COATING

200g dark chocolate, chopped

15g unsalted butter

1 heaped teaspoon golden syrup

50g white chocolate, chopped

YOU WILL ALSO NEED

40 x 26cm Swiss roll tin

disposable piping bag

MAKE THE SPONGE

1. Preheat the oven to 180°C/160°C fan/gas mark 4 and grease and line the baking tin with buttered baking parchment.

2. Tip the caster sugar into a large bowl or the bowl of stand mixer. Add the eggs and vanilla extract or paste and whisk on high for 2 minutes, until the mixture is pale, has trebled in volume and holds a firm ribbon trail when the whisk is lifted from the bowl.

3. Sift the flour, cocoa powder, baking powder and salt into the bowl and use a large metal spoon or rubber spatula to carefully fold the ingredients into the egg mixture, being careful not to knock out too much air. When the dry ingredients are almost completely incorporated, pour the melted butter around the edges of the mixture and fold in.

4. Carefully pour the cake mix into the prepared tin and gently spread it to the edges, again taking care not to knock out too much air. Bake for 7 minutes, until risen and spongy, then remove from the oven and leave to cool in the tin for 5 minutes before turning out onto a clean sheet of parchment. Peel off the top layer of parchment paper and trim the short edges of the sponge.

5. Starting at the long side nearest to you and using the parchment paper to help you, carefully roll up the cake into a tight roll with the parchment inside. Leave to cool.

FILL THE ROLL

6. While the cake is cooling, make the vanilla buttercream following the instructions on page 22.

7. When the sponge is completely cold, carefully unroll it. Use a palette knife to spread an even layer of buttercream over the surface and then re-roll it into a tight Swiss roll, using the parchment to help support it, but don't roll the paper into the roll this time. Pop the cake in the fridge for 30 minutes to firm up.

COAT THE CAKE AND CUT THE SLICES

8. Melt the dark chocolate in a heatproof bowl set over a pan of barely simmering water, making sure the bottom of the bowl doesn't touch the water, or in the microwave on a low setting. Stir until smooth, add the butter and golden syrup and stir to combine. Leave to cool for 5–10 minutes and then spoon the melted chocolate over the top of the cake so that it covers the top and sides evenly. Leave to set for 20 minutes.

9. Meanwhile, melt the white chocolate as above and cool for a couple of minutes. Spoon it into a disposable piping bag and snip off the end to make a fine point. Drizzle the white chocolate over the cooled dark chocolate and leave to set firm before cutting into 2cm slices to serve.

IF YOU DON'T HAVE A PIPING BAG YOU COULD USE A FREEZER BAG, TWISTING IT TIGHTLY AROUND THE WHITE CHOCOLATE AND SNIPPING OFF ONE CORNER TO MAKE A FINE POINT FOR DRIZZLING.

MALTED BROWNIES

MAKES 25

Brownies can be a little too chocolatey (if there is such a thing) for small children, so this recipe contains slightly less chocolate than normal brownies. There is, however, barley malt extract, which keeps the brownies moist and gooey without compromising on flavour. If you can't find barley malt extract you could also use date syrup.

150g dark chocolate (60–64% cocoa solids), broken into chunks
200g unsalted butter, diced
250g caster sugar
75g barley malt extract or date syrup
1 teaspoon vanilla extract
3 eggs, lightly beaten
125g plain flour
½ teaspoon baking powder
a pinch of salt
100g milk chocolate chips, optional
icing sugar, for dusting

YOU WILL ALSO NEED
1 x 23cm square cake tin

1. Preheat the oven to 180°C/160°C fan/gas mark 4 and grease and line the cake tin with buttered baking parchment.

2. Place the chocolate and butter in a heatproof bowl set over a pan of barely simmering water, making sure the bottom of the bowl doesn't touch the water. Melt slowly, stirring from time to time, until smooth. Remove from the heat and cool at room temperature for 5–10 minutes.

3. Add the caster sugar, barley malt extract or date syrup and vanilla extract to the melted chocolate and mix to combine. Add the eggs and mix until smooth. Sift the flour, baking powder and salt into the bowl and mix again until silky smooth. If you are using chocolate chips, fold them into the batter now.

4. Spoon the mixture into the prepared tin and level it with a spatula or the back of a spoon.

5. Bake for 25–30 minutes until slightly risen and a skewer inserted into the centre comes out with only a moist crumb attached. Leave in the tin to cool completely before dusting with icing sugar and cutting into squares to serve.

MINTY CHOCOLATE SANDWICH BISCUITS

MAKES 25–30 SANDWICHES

A slightly retro classic – this flavour combination is likely to appeal to adults as much as children! The sandwiches are half-dipped in chocolate but you can completely coat them if you prefer.

FOR THE BISCUITS
175g unsalted butter
125g caster sugar
1 teaspoon vanilla bean paste
1 egg, lightly beaten
225g plain flour, plus extra for dusting
40g cocoa powder
½ teaspoon bicarbonate of soda
a pinch of salt

FOR THE FILLING AND COATING
60g unsalted butter
100g icing sugar, sifted
1 tablespoon milk
a few drops of peppermint extract
150g dark chocolate (around 60% cocoa solids) or half milk and half dark chocolate
green nonpareils sprinkles

YOU WILL ALSO NEED
2 x baking sheets
5–6cm fluted square cutter

MAKE THE BISCUITS

1. Tip the butter, caster sugar and vanilla bean paste into a bowl or the bowl of a stand mixer and cream until pale and light. Scrape down the sides of the bowl, add the egg and mix to combine.

2. Sift the flour, cocoa powder, bicarbonate of soda and salt into the bowl and mix to combine without overworking the dough. Gather the dough into a ball, flatten it into a disc, wrap it in cling film and chill for about 2 hours until firm. Line the baking sheets with baking parchment.

3. Roll out the dough on a lightly floured work surface to 2–3mm thick and use the cutter to stamp out squares, re-rolling the excess to make more. Arrange on the prepared baking sheets and chill for 20 minutes. Preheat the oven to 180°C/160°C fan/gas mark 4.

4. Bake the biscuits for about 12 minutes, until firm. Leave to cool on the baking sheets.

FILL AND DIP THE SANDWICHES

5. Cream 50g of the butter until smooth and light. Gradually add the sifted icing sugar along with the milk and beat again until soft and thoroughly combined. Add the peppermint extract and mix again.

6. Spread the flat undersides of half the biscuits with buttercream. Sandwich with the remaining biscuits, flat sides facing, and press together gently. Chill for 20 minutes.

7. Melt the chocolate in a heatproof bowl set over a pan of barely simmering water, making sure the bottom of the bowl doesn't touch the water, or in the microwave on a low setting. Stir until smooth, add the remaining butter and stir again until combined. Remove from the heat and leave to cool for 10 minutes.

8. Take one of the biscuit sandwiches and, holding it horizontally, dip the bottom half in the chocolate and lay it on a clean sheet of parchment with the melted chocolate face up. Scatter with nonpareils sprinkles and leave in a cool place for the chocolate to set firm before serving.

FUNNY FACE SANDWICH BISCUITS

MAKES 20 SANDWICHES

Each one of these biscuits seems to have a slightly different expression, but all of them are happy! Be sure to use real malted milk powder and not a 'light' version, which will have less depth of flavour and often contains added chocolate powder.

FOR THE BISCUITS

175g unsalted butter

100g caster sugar

1 teaspoon vanilla vanilla bean paste or extract

1 egg, lightly beaten

1 tablespoon malt extract

250g plain flour, plus extra for dusting

50g malted milk powder

½ teaspoon baking powder

a pinch of salt

FOR THE FILLING

75g unsalted butter

1 teaspoon vanilla bean paste

150g icing sugar, sifted

1 tablespoon milk

12 teaspoons seedless raspberry jam or hazelnut chocolate spread

YOU WILL ALSO NEED

2 x baking sheets

5cm plain round cutter

skewer

MAKE THE BISCUITS

1. Cream the butter and caster sugar together until pale and light. Scrape down the sides of the bowl, add the vanilla extract and mix again to combine. Add the egg in 2 or 3 stages, mixing well between each addition. Add the malt extract and mix again to combine.

2. Sift the flour, malted milk powder, baking powder and salt into the bowl, mix to combine and bring the dough together smoothly. Scoop the dough into a ball, flatten it into a disc, wrap it in cling film and chill for about 2 hours until firm. Line the baking sheets with parchment paper.

3. Roll out the dough on a lightly dusted work surface to 2–3mm thick and use the cutter to stamp out as many discs as you can, re-rolling the offcuts to make more. Arrange on the prepared baking sheets and then use a skewer to stamp 2 eyes into each biscuit. Press the blunt edge of the cutter into the biscuits to give them each a mouth. Chill for 20 minutes. Preheat the oven to 180°C/160°C fan/gas mark 4.

4. Bake the biscuits for 12 minutes, until firm and lightly golden at the edges. Leave to cool on the baking sheets.

FILL THE SANDWICHES

5. Beat the softened butter until very pale and light. Add the vanilla and mix to combine. Gradually add the sifted icing sugar and milk and beat until smooth.

6. Spread the flat bottoms of half the biscuits with buttercream and the other half with jam. Sandwich the jam and buttercream biscuits together to serve.

ICED BUNS

Soft, slightly sweet dough topped with sweet, sticky icing and hundreds and thousands – like doughnuts, iced buns are impossible to resist. Fondant icing sugar is now available with added freeze-dried fruit powder, which not only gives a fantastic flavour, but natural colour, too.

FOR THE DOUGH

250ml whole milk

500g strong flour, plus extra for dusting

50g caster sugar

7g fast-action yeast

a large pinch of salt

1 egg, lightly beaten

50g unsalted butter

1 tablespoon sunflower oil, for greasing

FOR THE DECORATION

300g plain or freeze-dried raspberry fondant icing sugar

food-colouring pastes, optional

sugar sprinkles

YOU WILL ALSO NEED

2 × baking sheets

MAKE THE DOUGH

1. Heat the milk in a microwave or small pan over a low heat until it is hand hot.

2. Tip the flour into a large bowl or the bowl of a stand mixer fitted with a dough hook. Add the sugar, yeast and salt and mix to combine. Make a well in the middle of the dry ingredients and add the warm milk, beaten egg and butter and mix to combine to a rough dough. Either continue to knead in the mixer or turn out onto the work surface and knead for 5–10 minutes until the dough is soft, smooth and elastic. Shape into a smooth ball, place in a large, lightly oiled mixing bowl and cover loosely with cling film. Leave in a warm, draught-free spot in the kitchen for about 1 hour, or until the dough has doubled in size.

3. Tip the risen dough onto a lightly dusted work surface and knead for 30 seconds, then cut into 12–16 even-sized pieces and roll each one into finger or round buns, with the seals on the underside. Arrange 6 buns on each of the prepared baking sheets, leaving plenty of space between each one. Cover loosely with lightly oiled cling film and leave to prove for a further 45 minutes, or until doubled in size and the dough springs back when gently pressed with your fingertip. Preheat the oven to 200°C/180°C fan/gas mark 6.

4. Bake the buns for about 15 minutes, until golden brown, swapping the trays around halfway through cooking to ensure that they brown evenly. Leave to cool on the trays for 2–3 minutes and then transfer to a wire rack and leave until cold.

ICE THE BUNS

5. Mix the fondant icing sugar with 1–2 tablespoons cold water, until it becomes a spreadable paste that is thick enough to coat the top of the buns without dripping down the sides. Add a tiny drop of food colouring if required.

6. Spread the icing over the top of each bun using a palette knife and leave it to set for 5 minutes before scattering with sprinkles. Leave to set completely before serving.

YO-YO BISCUITS

MAKES 12–16

These crumbly, melt-in-the-mouth biscuits have a secret ingredient – custard powder. This not only gives them a wonderful colour, but a creamier flavour, too.

FOR THE BISCUITS

200g unsalted butter

75g icing sugar

200g plain flour

½ teaspoon baking powder

50g custard powder

a pinch of salt

1 teaspoon vanilla extract

2 tablespoons milk

16 strawberry laces

FOR THE VANILLLA BUTTERCREAM

75g unsalted butter

150g icing sugar

1 teaspoon vanilla extract

1 teaspoon milk

YOU WILL ALSO NEED

2 × baking sheets

MAKE THE BISCUITS

1. Cream the butter until really soft, light and pale. Sift the icing sugar into the bowl and mix again until smooth and thoroughly combined, then sift in the flour, baking powder, custard powder and a pinch of salt. Add the vanilla and milk and mix to bring the dough together. Cover with cling film and chill for 30 minutes until firm. Line the baking sheets with baking parchment.

2. Pinch off large, even, cherry sized balls of dough and roll them into neat balls. Arrange on the prepared baking sheets, leaving a little space between each one and slightly flattening the biscuits with your fingers. Chill for 20 minutes. Preheat the oven to 180°C/160°C fan/gas mark 4.

3. Press the tines of a fork into each biscuit to make criss-cross patterns and bake for about 12 minutes, until firm and golden at the edges. Leave to cool on the baking sheets.

MAKE THE BUTTERCREAM AND ASSEMBLE THE YO-YOS

4. Make the vanilla buttercream following the instructions on page 22.

5. Lay half the biscuits flat side up and spread them with buttercream. Sandwich with the rest of the biscuits, flat sides together, and then wind a strawberry lace around the middle of each sandwich to serve.

SAVOURY BAKES

CHEESE STRAWS

MAKES ABOUT 50

These couldn't be easier to make and are a crowd pleaser for children and adults. Poppy seeds add an extra crunch and the cayenne pepper and mustard powder a gentle hit of spice. They keep well and can be made up to 4 days before the party.

225g plain flour, plus extra for dusting
½ teaspoon cayenne pepper
½ teaspoon dry mustard powder
150g unsalted butter, chilled and diced
125g mature Cheddar, finely grated, plus 4 tablespoons
50g Parmesan, finely grated
2 tablespoons poppy seeds
a little milk, for brushing
salt and freshly ground black pepper

YOU WILL ALSO NEED

2 × baking sheets

STORE CHEESE STRAWS IN LAYERS IN AN AIRTIGHT CONTAINER, BETWEEN SHEETS OF WAXED PAPER OR BAKING PARCHMENT.

1. Sift the flour, cayenne pepper and mustard powder into a large bowl, season with salt and freshly ground black pepper and add the butter. Rub in the butter with your hands, lifting the mixture up and out of the bowl and gently pressing it between your fingertips as it drops back in. You can also do this step in a food-processor using the pulse button.

2. Add the 125g grated Cheddar, the Parmesan and poppy seeds and mix or pulse until the dough starts to come together into a ball. Tip onto a work surface and knead very lightly to combine. Flatten into a neat square block, wrap in cling film and chill for 30 minutes.

3. Preheat the oven to 200°C/180°C fan/gas mark 6 and line the baking sheets with baking parchment.

4. Roll out half the dough on a lightly dusted work surface to a neat rectangle about 6–7mm thick. Cut into thin, finger-width strips and arrange on one of the prepared baking sheets, leaving a little space between each one. Repeat with the remaining dough.

5. Brush the cheese straws with a little milk, scatter with the remaining 4 tablespoons grated cheese and bake for about 12 minutes until golden. Cool on the baking sheets before serving.

CHEESE CRACKER SANDWICHES

MAKES 24 SANDWICHES

*These crisp crackers and the herby filling can be prepared in advance.
They can then be sandwiched together up to 2 hours before serving.*

FOR THE CRACKERS

225g plain flour, plus extra for dusting

2 teaspoons baking powder

2 teaspoons caster sugar

½ teaspoon salt, plus extra for sprinkling

150g unsalted butter, chilled and diced

2–3 tablespoons ice-cold water

2 teaspoons cider vinegar

1 egg yolk

1 tablespoon milk

FOR THE FILLING

15g chives

150g cream cheese

freshly ground black pepper

YOU WILL ALSO NEED

2 x baking sheets

5cm fluted rectangular cutter

1. Sift the flour, baking powder, sugar and salt into a large bowl. Add the chilled diced butter and rub it in with your hands, lifting the mixture up and out of the bowl and gently pressing it between your fingertips as it drops back in. You can also do this in the food-processor using the pulse button. Make a well in the centre of the mixture.

2. In a small bowl, mix the ice-cold water with the cider vinegar and pour this into the large bowl. Use a round-bladed knife to mix together and then bring the dough together with your hands, knead lightly into a smooth ball and flatten into a disc. Wrap in cling film and chill for 30 minutes. Line the baking sheets with parchment paper.

3. Roll out the dough on a lightly dusted work surface to 2mm thick. Use the cutter to stamp out as many rectangles as you can and arrange them on the prepared baking sheets. Re-roll the scraps to stamp out more crackers. Prick each one 3 times with a fork and chill again for 20 minutes. Preheat the oven to 180°C/160°C fan/gas mark 4.

4. Mix the egg yolk with the milk and brush the top of each cracker. Sprinkle with a little salt and bake for about 12 minutes, until crisp and golden. Leave to cool on the baking sheets.

5. Finely snip the chives into a bowl with the cream cheese and season with black pepper.

6. Flip over half the crackers and spread the flat undersides with a little cream cheese mixture. Sandwich with the remaining crackers, flat sides together, and serve.

HERBY SAUSAGE ROLLS

MAKES 30

It seems that no matter how many sausage rolls you make they will always be eaten and these little bite-sized ones are no exception. Be sure to use good-quality sausagemeat and all-butter puff pastry for best results.

450g good-quality sausagemeat

4 large spring onions, trimmed and finely chopped

2 tablespoons finely chopped parsley

1 tablespoon finely chopped sage

2 teaspoons Dijon mustard

375g all-butter ready-roll puff pastry

1 tablespoon poppy or sesame seeds

2 tablespoons milk, for brushing

salt and freshly ground black pepper

plain flour, for dusting

tomato ketchup, to serve

YOU WILL ALSO NEED

2 x baking sheets

PREPARE AND FREEZE ON TRAYS BEFORE BAKING, OR COOK AND FREEZE IN PLASTIC CONTAINERS. DEFROST AND REHEAT THOROUGHLY BEFORE SERVING.

1. Put the sausagemeat in a mixing bowl with the spring onions, parsley, sage and Dijon mustard and season with salt and freshly ground black pepper. Mix together with clean hands until thoroughly combined.

2. Line the baking sheets with baking parchment. Lightly dust the work surface with plain flour and roll out the pastry to a neat 30–31cm square, roughly 2mm thick. Trim the right-hand edge to neaten it.

3. Divide the sausage into 3 portions and use damp hands to shape one-third into a long thin sausage that's the same length as the pastry and roughly the same thickness as, and no thicker than, a chipolata. Lay the sausage along the right-hand side of the pastry and brush the pastry along the left edge of the sausagement with milk. Roll the pastry over the sausage to encase it. Cut out 1 long sausage roll with the seal on the underside. Repeat to make 3 long sausage rolls, then trim the ends and cut into 3cm mini rolls.

4. Arrange the mini sausage rolls on the prepared baking sheets, brush with milk and use a sharp knife to cut 3 slashes into the top of each one. Scatter poppy or sesame seeds over the top and chill for 30 minutes. Preheat the oven to 220°C/200°C fan/gas mark 7.

5. Bake the sausage rolls for about 25 minutes, until the pastry is crisp and golden brown. Serve warm or cold, with ketchup.

HIDDEN HOT DOGZ

MAKES 20

If your children are good eaters, try frying some thinly sliced onion in a little olive oil until soft and caramelised and add this to the buns with the sausages or serve alongside.

FOR THE ROLLS

250g strong white flour, plus extra for dusting

1½ teaspoons fast-action yeast

1 teaspoon caster sugar

a good pinch of salt

125ml milk, plus extra for brushing

25g unsalted butter

1 egg yolk

1 tablespoon sesame seeds

FOR THE FILLING

20 good-quality cocktail sausages

1 teaspoon sunflower oil

TO SERVE

tomato ketchup

American-style mustard

YOU WILL ALSO NEED

baking sheet

small baking tray

1. Tip the flour into a large bowl or the bowl of a stand mixer. Add the yeast, sugar and salt, mix to combine and make a well in the centre.

2. Heat the milk in the microwave or in a small pan over a low heat until it is hand hot. Stir in the butter and pour the mixture into the dry ingredients along with the egg yolk. Mix to combine, then tip the dough onto a lightly floured work surface or switch to a dough hook and knead for about 5 minutes, until silky smooth. Shape the dough into a neat ball and place it in a large bowl, cover with cling film and leave in a warm, draught-free part of the kitchen for about 1 hour, or until doubled in size.

3. Meanwhile, preheat the oven to 200°C/180°C fan/gas mark 6 and line the baking tray with foil. Tip the sausages onto the tray, drizzle with the oil and toss to coat. Cook for 20–25 minutes, until starting to brown nicely. Leave to cool on the tray. Line a baking sheet with baking parchment.

4. Turn out the proved dough onto a very lightly floured work surface and knead for 30 seconds to knock back the air. Divide into 20 even-sized pieces and roll out each piece to a rectangle roughly 3mm thick.

5. Place a cocktail sausage in the middle of each rectangle and brush around it with a little milk. Fold the dough around the sausage and roll it over so that the sausage is completely encased and the seal is underneath. Arrange on the prepared baking sheet, leaving a little space between each roll, and cover loosely with cling film. Leave to prove for about 40 minutes, until the dough is light and puffy.

6. Brush the proved rolls with a little milk to glaze and use a sharp knife to slash the top of each roll 3 times, cutting all the way down to the sausage. Sprinkle with sesame seeds and bake for about 20 minutes, until golden brown. Drizzle with ketchup and American-style mustard and serve.

LUIS' PIZZA MUFFINS

MAKES 12

Everyone likes pizza, don't they? Well here's a fun recipe for pizza muffins.
You can make the dough a day ahead and keep it in the fridge until needed.

FOR THE DOUGH

500g strong white flour, plus extra for dusting

1 teaspoon fine salt

7g fast-action yeast

1 tablespoon extra virgin olive oil

2 teaspoons dried oregano

FOR THE FLAVOURING

6 tablespoons tomato ketchup

100g thinly sliced pepperoni

30g fresh basil leaves

130g grated mozzarella

2 tablespoons extra virgin olive oil

1 tablespoon green or red pesto

YOU WILL ALSO NEED

12-hole muffin tin

12 tulip muffin cases, or make your own with squares
of parchment paper

MAKE THE DOUGH

1. Place all the ingredients for the dough and 220ml water
in a mixing bowl or the bowl of a stand mixer fitted with
a dough hook. Mix on low or using your hands until the
ingredients come together. Add more water as required
until all the dry ingredients are incorporated – it should be
a soft, sticky dough. Mix or knead for around 8 minutes.

2. Place the dough in an oiled bowl and cover with cling
film. Leave to prove for 1 hour, or until doubled in size.
Alternatively, make the dough the day before and place it
in the fridge to prove slowly overnight. Line the muffin tin
with the tulip cases or squares of parchment paper.

3. Tip the proved dough onto a well-floured work surface
and knock it back slightly by flattening it with your hand.
Roll it out to a rectangle about 60 × 30cm, with one of
the long edges nearest you. Press the edges down lightly
to secure the dough to the work surface.

FILL AND ROLL THE MUFFINS

4. Spread a stripe of ketchup along the long edge nearest
you and a second parallel stripe about halfway up. Top
the ketchup strips with pepperoni. Sprinkle the basil and
mozzarella all over the dough, leaving about 3cm uncovered
at the long edge furthest away from you.

5. Starting at the long edge nearest you, roll the dough
tightly into a giant roll and then cut it into 12 equal slices.
Roll each piece in flour and place in the muffin cases with
the spirals facing up. Cover the tray with cling film and leave
to prove for about 1 hour, until puffed up and doubled in
size. Preheat the oven to 200°C/180°C fan/gas mark 6.

6. Bake for about 25 minutes, until golden, then transfer to
a wire rack rack set over a tray. Mix together the olive oil
and pesto and drizzle each muffin while they're still hot.

SWEETCORN & SMOKED CHEESE MUFFINS

MAKES 10–12

Bake these savoury muffins in mini loaf tin paper cases, which are now available in most large supermarket baking aisles. The mustard and cayenne pepper add flavour rather than heat, but a scattering of finely chopped jalapeño slices would give these muffins a spicy kick.

25g unsalted butter

150ml soured cream

100ml milk

2 eggs

275g plain flour

3 teaspoons baking powder

½ teaspoon dry mustard powder

½ teaspoon cayenne pepper

150g smoked Cheddar, grated

200g sweetcorn kernels

4 spring onions, trimmed and chopped

1 tablespoon snipped chives

1 tablespoon finely chopped jalapeño peppers, optional

a pinch of salt

freshly ground black pepper

YOU WILL ALSO NEED

1 x 12-hole muffin tin or 12 mini loaf tin cases

paper muffin cases, optional

baking tray, optional

1. Preheat the oven to 200°C/180°C fan/gas mark 6. Line the muffin tin with paper cases or arrange the mini loaf cases on a baking tray.

2. Melt the butter in a small saucepan over a low heat or in a heatproof jug in the microwave and leave to cool slightly. Add the soured cream, milk and eggs and mix well to combine.

3. Sift the flour, baking powder, mustard powder and cayenne pepper into a large mixing bowl. Add the grated cheese, sweetcorn, spring onions, chives and jalapeños, if using, season with the salt and freshly ground black pepper and mix to combine. Make a well in the middle of the dry ingredients, pour in the egg mixture and use a large metal spoon to gently fold in the mixture until only just combined.

4. Divide the mixture between the paper cases and bake for about 20 minutes, until golden brown and well risen.

4-FLAVOUR BREADSTICKS

MAKES 35–40

This clever little recipe makes four different, deliciously flavoured breadsticks.

FOR THE DOUGH

350g strong white bread flour

7g fast-action yeast

½ teaspoon salt

150ml milk

2 tablespoons olive oil

FOR THE FLAVOURINGS

6 rashers smoked streaky bacon

1 rounded teaspoon smoked paprika

2–3 teaspoons yeast extract

1 tablespoon sesame seeds

2 tablespoons pesto

3 rounded tablespoons finely grated Parmesan

TO SERVE

hummus

guacamole

YOU WILL ALSO NEED

2 × baking sheets

small baking tray

MAKE THE DOUGH

1. Tip the flour into a large bowl or the bowl of a stand mixer, add the yeast and salt, mix to combine and make a well in the centre.

2. Heat the milk with 100ml water in the microwave or in a small pan over a low heat until hand hot. Add the olive oil and pour the mixture into the dry ingredients. Mix to combine and then knead the dough for about 5 minutes

until silky smooth, either using the mixer fitted with a dough hook or by hand on a work surface. Shape the dough into a ball and place it in a large bowl. Cover with cling film and leave in a warm, draught-free part of the kitchen for about 1 hour, or until doubled in size.

FLAVOUR AND BAKE THE BREADSTICKS

3. Meanwhile, preheat the oven to 200°C/180°C fan/gas mark 6 and line a small baking tray with foil. Line the baking sheets with parchment paper. Lay the bacon rashers on the tray and bake for 10–12 minutes, until crisp. Drain on kitchen paper and leave until cold, then finely chop and mix with the smoked paprika.

4. Knead the proved dough on a lightly dusted work surface for 30 seconds to knock back any air. Divide into 4 even portions.

5. Flatten 1 portion of dough into a disc and spoon the paprika bacon bits on top. Fold them into the dough and knead thoroughly to incorporate. Roll out to a rough rectangle about 3mm thick and use a long-bladed knife or pasta wheel to cut the dough into 1cm strips. Roll each strip on the work surface to round off the edges and arrange on the prepared baking sheet.

6. Flatten another portion of dough into a disc and top with the yeast extract. Knead to incorporate and cut into breadsticks. Scatter the sesame seeds onto a board and roll the breadsticks in them, smoothing off the edges. Arrange on the baking sheet and cover loosely with cling film.

7. Knead the pesto into the third dough portion, roll and shape as above and arrange on a second baking sheet. Knead 2 tablespoons of the grated Parmesan into the final piece of dough, cut and shape into breadsticks and scatter with more Parmesan. Lay on the baking sheet and cover the tray loosely with cling film. Leave all the breadsticks to prove for 30 minutes, until puffy.

8. Bake the proved breadsticks for 12–15 minutes, until golden brown. Leave to cool on the trays and serve with hummus and guacamole.

CHEESY LITTLE SCONES

MAKES 20

Scones take very little time to prepare and are best eaten on the day of making. Although these cheese scones don't really need to be filled, they would be delicious served with a little butter or perhaps cream cheese.

300g plain flour, plus extra for dusting

3 teaspoons baking powder

heaped ½ teaspoon mustard powder

¼–½ teaspoon cayenne pepper

a pinch of salt

60g unsalted butter, chilled and diced

100g Cheddar, finely grated, plus 1 tablespoon

25g Parmesan, finely grated

4 spring onions, finely chopped

100g buttermilk

125ml milk, plus 1 tablespoon for glazing

freshly ground black pepper

YOU WILL ALSO NEED

baking sheet

5cm round cutter

ALTHOUGH PERFECT FOR TEA PARTIES, CHEESY SCONES ARE ALSO DELICIOUS SERVED ALONGSIDE A BOWL OF STEAMING SOUP OR POPPED INTO A LUNCHBOX.

1. Preheat the oven to 220°C/200°C fan/gas mark 7. Line the baking sheet with baking parchment.

2. Sift the flour, baking powder, mustard powder and cayenne pepper into a large mixing bowl. Season well with freshly ground black pepper and a pinch of salt and add the butter, rubbing it into the dry ingredients with your fingertips. When there are only very small specks of butter still visible, add the 100g grated Cheddar, the Parmesan and spring onions. Mix to combine.

3. Make a well in the centre of the bowl and pour in the buttermilk and 125ml milk. Use a round-bladed knife to mix to a rough dough, then use your hands to very lightly bring the mixture into a ball. Tip it onto the work surface and knead for no more than 10 seconds, then flatten to a disc about 2cm thick and stamp out rounds, re-rolling the offcuts to make more. Arrange on the prepared baking sheet, leaving a little space between each one.

4. Brush the tops of the scones with a little milk, scatter with the remaining cheeses and bake for about 12 minutes, until well risen and golden brown. Cool on a wire rack and eat while still slightly warm.

FISH 'N' CHIPS BISCUITS

SERVES 12

These savoury little biscuits have a hint of salt and vinegar. Note that the vinegar for the coating has a weight, rather than liquid, measurement. It will be absorbed by the cornflour to make a slightly damp seasoning powder.

FOR THE DOUGH

250g plain flour, plus extra for dusting

150g unsalted butter, chilled and diced

25g Parmesan, finely grated

1 egg yolk

2 tablespoons ice-cold water

2 teaspoons malt vinegar

salt and freshly ground black pepper

FOR THE COATING

25g malt vinegar

50g cornflour

a good pinch of salt

YOU WILL ALSO NEED

1 small fish-shaped cutter

2 × baking sheets

MAKE THE BISCUIT DOUGH

1. Tip the flour into a large mixing bowl and add the butter. Cut the butter into the flour using a round-bladed knife until the pieces are well coated with flour and at least halved in size. Switch to your hands to rub in the butter, lifting the mixture up and out of the bowl and gently pressing it between your fingertips as it drops back in. When there are only tiny pieces of butter still visible, add the grated Parmesan, season with salt and freshly ground black pepper and mix to combine. Make a well in the middle of the mixture.

2. In a small bowl mix together the egg yolk, ice-cold water and malt vinegar and then pour the mixture into the dry ingredients. Use the round-bladed knife to combine. Use your hands to bring the dough together into a ball, flatten it into a disc, wrap it in cling film and chill for 1 hour until firm.

BAKE AND COAT THE BISCUITS

3. Mix the weighed malt vinegar with the cornflour and salt until you have a damp powder. Line the baking sheets with parchment paper.

4. Roll out the dough on a lightly floured work surface to 2mm thick. Use the cutter to stamp out 12–16 fish-shaped biscuits and arrange them on the prepared baking sheets. Gather the scraps together into a ball and re-roll them. Use a long-bladed knife to cut the dough into finger-sized chips and arrange alongside the fish. Chill for 20 minutes. Preheat the oven to 180°C/160°C fan/gas mark 4.

5. Bake the biscuits for about 12 minutes, until crisp and golden brown. Allow to cool on the tray for 5 minutes and then transfer to a large mixing bowl.

6. Add the vinegary cornflour and gently mix with your hands. The biscuits will be lightly coated in the cornflour seasoning. Shake off any excess cornflour and leave to cool on a wire rack before serving in mini paper cones.

CHETNA'S MINI BAKED NAAN BITES

MAKES 14

I love to do lots of baking to make my kids' parties special. It is easy to buy ready made food, but it's not always that healthy. My kids love naan so I decided to make these mini baked versions, which are a great portion size for kids. The crispy base is topped with a thin layer of tomato and some cheesy potatoes, and finished with mozzarella and thin slices of tomato. It's really easy, healthy food and kids love the simple flavours.

FOR THE DOUGH

250g plain flour
½ teaspoon salt
1 teaspoon fast-action yeast
2 tablespoons natural yogurt
1 tablespoon olive oil
100ml warm water

FOR THE TOPPING

100g tomato purée
2 boiled potatoes, grated
6 tablespoons grated Cheddar
½ teaspoon salt
¼ teaspoon black pepper
200g mozzarella pearls
2–3 firm tomatoes, thinly sliced

YOU WILL ALSO NEED

2–3 baking sheets

1. In a large bowl, mix together the flour, salt, yeast, yogurt and oil. Slowly add the warm water and mix well until the dough comes together. You might need a little more or less water. Place on a lightly oiled surface and knead for 5–7 minutes, then place in a lightly oiled bowl, cover with cling film and leave to prove for 1–1½ hours.

2. Mix together the grated boiled potatoes, Cheddar, salt and pepper and mix well. Preheat the oven to 200°C/180°C fan/gas mark 6.

3. Knead the proved dough to get rid of all the air and divide it into 14 portions, each one weighing roughly 30g. Roll out each portion to a 24cm circle and spread them with tomato purée. Spread about 1 tablespoon of the potato mix onto each one and top with 2 or 3 mozzarella pearls and a few slices of tomato.

4. Bake for 10–12 minutes, until cooked through, and serve warm.

INDEX

ACKNOWLEDGEMENTS

Annie Rigg would like to say an enormous thank you to:

Lola Milne – she's a pocket-rocket-power-house-cake-maker-
assistant-extraordinaire. She kept the wheels turning,
the buttercream mountain topped up and never stopped smiling
throughout the photoshoot for this book.

Debby Lewis-Harrison for being a total joy and bringing the party
to life with her wonderful pictures.

Jen Haslam for her beautiful props, wonderfully imaginative set ups
and for covering the studio with confetti and streamers.

Louise Leffler for her wonderful design, art direction
and boundless enthusiasm.

Caroline McArthur and Sarah Hammond for their combined wisdom,
patience and all round brilliance.

Hodder & Stoughton and Love Productions would like
to thank the following people for their contributions to this book:
Annie Rigg, Caroline McArthur, Louise Leffler, Debby Lewis-
Harrison, Jennifer Haslam, Nicky Ross, Sarah Hammond, Alasdair
Oliver, Kate Brunt, Claudette Morris, Joanna Seaton, Auriol Bishop,
Anna Beattie, Rupert Frisby, Jane Treasure, Claire Emerson.

First published in Great Britain in 2016 by Hodder & Stoughton
An Hachette UK company

1

Copyright © Love Productions Limited 2016

Additional recipes: p92 Holly's Camping Cake copyright
© Holly Bell 2016, p121 Miranda's Milk Chocolate Brownie Cake
copyright © Miranda Gore Browne 2016, p126 Ian's Banoffee
Cake copyright © Ian Cumming 2016, p143 Frances's Star Baker
Medal Biscuits copyright © Frances Quinn 2016, p164 Cathryn's
Moustache-pop Biscuits copyright © Cathryn Dresser 2016,
p178 Richard's Funfetti Shortbread Sandwich Biscuits copyright
© Richard Burr 2016, p204 Luis' Pizza Muffins copyright © Luis
Troyano 2016, p216 Chetna's Mini Baked Naan Bites copyright
© Chetna Makan 2016.

Photography & Design Copyright © Hodder & Stoughton
Ltd 2016

Additional photography copyright © David Loftus p92,
copyright © Laura Edwards p121, copyright © Ian Cumming p127,
copyright © Georgia Glynn Smith/David Smith p164,
copyright © John Moore/Birkbeck, University of London p179,
copyright © Luis Troyano p204, copyright © Keith James p217.

A CIP catalogue record for this title is available from the
British Library

Hardback ISBN 978 1 473 61564 9
Ebook ISBN 978 1 473 61565 6

Editorial Director: Nicky Ross
Editor: Sarah Hammond
Project Editor: Caroline McArthur
Designer: Louise Leffler
Photographer: Debby Lewis-Harrison
Food Stylist: Annie Rigg
Props Stylist: Jennifer Haslam
Illustrator: Kuo Kang Chen

Typeset in Gill Sans

Printed and bound in Italy by L.E.G.O. Spa

Hodder & Stoughton policy is to use papers that are natural,
renewable and recyclable products and made from wood grown
in sustainable forests. The logging and manufacturing processes
are expected to conform to the environmental regulations of
the country of origin.

Hodder & Stoughton Ltd
Carmelite House
50 Victoria Embankment
London EC4Y 0DZ

www.hodder.co.uk